Solid Foundation Sermon Starters

MINOR
PROPHETS

Solid Foundation Sermon Starters

MINOR PROPHETS

*Blueprints for 28 messages
built upon God's Word*

Loren D. Deckard

Cincinnati, Ohio

All Scripture quotations, unless otherwise indicated, are taken from the HOLY BIBLE, NEW INTERNATIONAL VERSION®. NIV®. Copyright © 1973, 1978, 1984 by International Bible Society. Used by permission of Zondervan Publishing House. All rights reserved.

Cover design by Grannan Graphic Design LTD

Interior design by Robert E. Korth

Solid Foundation is an imprint from
The Standard Publishing Company, Cincinnati, Ohio.
A division of Standex International Corporation.
06 05 04 03 02 01 00 99   5 4 3 2 1

Contents

Introduction

Why would one ever want to preach from the writings of men who were never successful? They never built big churches, and they weren't noted for the success of their evangelistic efforts. They didn't design programs to meet people's needs, and they didn't write great how-to books.

Perhaps, like me, you have turned to the Minor Prophets only for grist for the mill of complaint about contemporary sinfulness. It is easy to compare the injustices of the day of Amos or the materialism of the day of Haggai to almost any generation.

However, in more recent years I have learned to see that these ancient preachers faced the ills of their days with insightful doctrinal statements, and it was then that I began to enjoy preaching the great doctrines of the prophets.

The sermons in this book will not follow the typical pattern of complaint about human sinfulness, God's warning about punishment, and the offer of safety if the people repent. While this is a pattern that is repeated several times in the prophetic literature, there is much more to be seen in their prophecies

The messages of the prophets ring through the centuries, and it is as if Solomon were saying again, "There is nothing new under the sun" (Ecclesiastes 1:9). Amos spoke out against the growing disparity between the rich and poor and the injustice accompanying it. During his time, worship activity was high, but the faith of the people was superficial. They valued prosperity more than righteousness. Kings of both Judah and Israel enjoyed popularity as the borders were extended to compare to the days of David and Solomon—but they did not know God!

While Amos was preaching in Israel, three young men were being prepared to follow him: Hosea in Israel, and Isaiah and Micah in Judah. Amos preached in the days of peace and prosperity as Assyria and Syria pulled back to lick their wounds (about 760–750 B.C.). These other three prophets followed him and preached in the days when the effects of the unrighteousness of Israel and Judah were beginning to become more evident in the crumbling of the nations.

Highway robbery, murder, and vice were prevalent in Hosea's day. There was pluralism as people worshiped the gods of other nations. Hosea's message centered on the broken heart of God when his people went after other gods. Courts accepted bribes. Leaders exhibited moral corruption in their personal lives. The nation deceived itself by thinking that its wealth would protect it. How could anything be seriously wrong with a nation enjoying such a strong economy? The prophet Hosea, whose own heart had been broken, was chosen to speak to a people who were breaking God's heart with their materialism, pluralism, and relativism.

7

Isaiah and Micah continued to preach to the southern kingdom during the last quarter of the eighth century, after Israel had fallen to Assyria. The southern kingdom was filled with greed and immoral behavior. Soothsaying, witchcraft, and superstition were the order of the day. In the midst of all this, Isaiah and Micah presented their messianic prophecies, which were not to be fulfilled for more than seven centuries.

Jonah learned of the interest of God in non-Jewish people, probably also during the eighth century. In the seventh century Habakkuk learned of God's watchfulness over all nations, and the message of God to Habakkuk began to be realized in the time of Zephaniah and Nahum.

After the exile in Babylon we begin to hear again from Minor Prophets. Haggai and Zechariah brought God's message to the people in the days of the rebuilding of the temple, which was dedicated in 515 B.C. Then, in the fifth century, before there was silence for four centuries prior to the coming of the Messiah, Joel and Malachi brought God's message to a people who, like their forebears, were more interested in their own prosperity, superstition, formal or professional religion, and immoral behavior than in God's things and God's ways.

The striking thing about the Minor Prophets is that their real message for today is not found just at the juncture of the immorality of their day with the immorality of ours. Rather, the most powerful messages are to be found in the sound, timeless doctrines. These are doctrines of God, of revelation, of righteousness, of good and evil, of worship, and of redemption.

Into a culture poised on the brink of a new millennium, a culture starved for the security of something to believe in, come the voices of the prophets. The truth and power of their message is not dimmed one bit by the centuries through which it has passed but cries out again with renewed vigor and speaks to this age! Study until you know the prophets, then preach their great doctrines!

It is advisable to read the entire prophetic book before studying the sermons on that book. This will give a sense of the prophet before looking more specifically at his message. Several sources I would recommend for further study of the Minor Prophets are Thomas E. McComiskey, ed., *The Minor Prophets: An Exegetical and Expository Commentary* (3 vols., Grand Rapids: Baker Book House, 1992–98); Kyle M. Yates, *Preaching From the Prophets* (Nashville: Broadman, 1942); and R. Laird Harris, Gleason L. Archer, Jr., and Bruce K. Waltke, eds., *Theological Wordbook of the Old Testament* (2 vols., Chicago: Moody Press, 1980).

Knowing God's Attributes

Various Passages

As our kids grew up they learned that their parents were fairly complex. When they were babies, we were quite one dimensional in our relationship to them. But as they became more mobile and exercised their curiosity, they began to see another dimension of their parents. There was the occasional, "No! You may not do that. It will hurt you" or "It will break your sister's doll." Full affirmation began to give way to occasional boundaries or even disapproval.

This continued to progress until they were teenagers. By this time they had been introduced to anger, worry, and fear as well as affirmation, affection, faithfulness, pride, and expectation. They became quite good at choosing their behavior based on which aspect of our complex personalities would be elicited by a given action.

These multifaceted personalities are normal and healthy. Living in such a complex emotional environment prepares children for a complex world. Indeed, children who grow up never receiving anything but affirmation and tenderness are ill prepared for a world in which they will not always receive such positive responses.

McComiskey, in his commentary on Zechariah, notes that people need to know the various aspects of God's character so they will know what to expect in response to their various behaviors and how to make behavioral decisions accordingly. In our "feel good" age, people often exhibit a one-dimensional view of God. He is the God who saves by grace, a free gift. Then they behave and talk as if there are few if any expectations of those who have this saving faith.

Proposition: God is a Father with a complex personality.

Zeph (3 Chapters)

I. GOD EXPERIENCES WRATH (ZEPHANIAH 2:1, 2).

A. In spite of what an old Christian song claims, God will not always say, "Well done!" The messages of the prophets clearly describe God's wrath in response to the behavior of his children.

B. On one occasion a sixteen-year-old child of ours decided to "hang out" at a local convenience store after being specifically and clearly told this was not permitted. I drove to the store so angry that I trusted myself only to say to her, "Get in the car!" The next morning she said, "You scared me, Dad. I've never seen you that angry." "Good!" I responded, "You need to know your behavior can make me that angry."

C. We also need to know that our behavior can make God angry. The fear of that anger may be what saves us from self-destruction.

II. GOD IS LONG-SUFFERING AND FORGIVING (HOSEA 11:3, 4; 14:1-9).

A. As angry as God can get, he can still forgive. As devastating as the actions of his wrath can be, the patience of his long-suffering can outstrip them. The same God whose wrath is heard in Zephaniah sends his love in Hosea.

B. After a wordless drive home from the convenience store, our daughter went to her room. Soon she came to the family room, where her mother and I were. She explained that she had been at the store with a friend who was running away from home. After a bit of conversation, we let her take the car to bring her friend home, with the understanding that we would call the girl's parents to explain where she was and that she was safe.

C. The story is longer, but the point is this: Our complex personalities, and the fact that our daughter understood their complexities, permitted her to be afraid of my wrath and at the same time be able to say to me, "My friend is in trouble." She knew there was another part of her parents that could hear and respond without anger. She depended on this. Likewise, you can depend on God's complex personality to shore up your quaking ship of life, for God is strong enough to be angry and tender enough to help.

III. GOD IS FAITHFUL (MALACHI 2:4, 5).

A. God is still faithful to his covenant with Levi. When I have faith in God, it is a decision on my part based on something I see in him. But the faithfulness of God is a quality of his character that stands apart from me or anyone else. God is faithful! He will keep his word.

B. One Friday night one of our children, age sixteen, came home about eleven and joined us in the kitchen, the family meeting place. She leaned against the wall with a sigh, slid to the floor, and said, "Boy, it's good to be home. I've been to three friends' homes tonight, and in every one I heard bickering, fighting, and hatefulness. I knew I wouldn't have to listen to that here."

C. We were faithful to a standard of family life upon which she could depend. This made home a safe place.

CONCLUSION

There are many other attributes of God we could talk about, but these will suffice to make the point that God has a genuine personality, not at all one dimensional, but complex. God is complex enough to meet our varied needs for love, blessing, discipline, guidance, assurance, and so on. Let us keep learning more and more of God's grand personality!

The View From the Crushed Heart

Hosea 4:1-9; 6:4-6; 7:8-15; 11:8; 14:1, 2

Hosea, our prophet for today, preached to the northern kingdom while Isaiah and Micah preached to the southern kingdom late in the eighth century. Amos had gone before him, preaching to Israel during her days of prosperity in the earlier part of the century.

While Amos had thundered the wrath of God against the injustice, materialism, and empty religion of his people, Hosea's words alternate between the dewy wetness of the tear-filled eye and the strong resolve that cannot condone sin. As a result, he opened new insights into the knowledge of what God is like.

As Amos had prophesied, the heyday of the Israelites could not last. While their priests continued false religion and corruption, a weakened throne recognized the handwriting on the wall and tried to save them from Assyria by making alliances with Damascus and Egypt. Things they had counted on were beginning to show their weakness, and their security was slipping away.

To this hour came a prophet of God who can help us, in a way no other has, to understand God. While Amos helped us see the broad nature of Israel's corruption and covered a number of great themes, Hosea plumbs the depths of a single theme: the perfect love of God for a rebellious, corrupt, and deliberately sinful people. He does so by relating the story of his own love life, a story that becomes a living image before our mind's eye and helps us to understand God's love in a way that words alone cannot express.

It was the broken heart of Hosea, still loving Gomer, that was able to understand the love of God's broken heart. It was through the eyes of this heart that he was able to woo the people of God to come back to him.

Proposition: The broken heart can most clearly understand and communicate the heart of God.

I. THE BROKEN HEART CAN MOVE BEYOND RETALIATION.

    A. Amos saw the sin and injustice of Israel. His anger was kindled, and he wrote in words that rang with the thunder of wrath. It was a stern, unbending justice and wrath that he pronounced on a selfish and uncaring people.

    B. In contrast, Hosea pled, exhorted, and courted the love of the people from the perspective of a loving and brokenhearted God. While justice demanded that the consequences of sin be met, the loving heart took no pleasure in this and grieved its necessity.

C. The crushed heart can no longer exist on platitudes and clichés about love. All is stripped away to lay naked one's true character and motivations. Then real discipline can be selflessly applied.

II. THE BROKEN HEART CAN HATE THE SIN AND LOVE THE SINNER.

A. Hosea 6:4 exhibits unspeakable tenderness toward the sinner: "What can I do with you, Ephraim? What can I do with you, Judah?" The lover's heart can cry out with a tender plea of helplessness. The helplessness is felt when one remembers the love held for the unfaithful partner or child. By seeing how Hosea could feel this way about Gomer, we can better understand God's love for us, even in our worst moments of sinfulness.

B. Hosea 4:1-9 shows unspeakable indignation over sin and ingratitude. If your heart has ever been crushed by a loved one, you know that one moment you can cry out for return and at another you can vent anger at the behavior. So it is with God and his people. As the prophet exclaims, "Ephraim is joined to idols; leave him alone! Even when their drinks are gone, they continue their prostitution; their rulers dearly love shameful ways" (4:17, 18).

III. THE BROKEN HEART UNDERSTANDS THE LIMITS OF LOVE.

A. The intertwined stories of Hosea's life and of the relationship between God and his people, Israel, make it clear that the lover cannot remake the object of love into the lover's image. Perhaps this is the primary reason human beings enjoy free will. God, loving us enough to die for us, will not attempt to take it out of our hands and force us to be what he wants us to be.

B. If you have ever asked a toddler to come to you, you know how much more joy there is in holding the toddler who gladly comes into your arms than in holding the one who doesn't want to be there, squirming and wiggling until you let go. Like Hosea and like God, we must wait for the ones we love to respond to our love.

CONCLUSION

The heart that has been broken can most clearly understand and communicate the heart of God. God waits for us, unwilling to force us into what he wants us to be. He waits, loving us even while hating some of our behavior. God waits, not willing to retaliate against us for our sin but knowing the consequences that must be paid. And God grieves our willfulness, our selfishness, our thoughtlessness, as we turn from him to pursue life without him. Search your heart in the times it is broken, and find there the heart of God.

Through the Eyes of God

Hosea

"If you could just see things as I do!" How often have we thought that when we heard someone bragging about their kids or skills, or bemoaning the fact that no one cares about them? [Briefly review the story of Hosea's marriage, the birth of their children, and the buying back of Gomer from Hosea 1–3.]

Having in mind the story of Hosea, let's try to see things through his eyes. This is Hosea's value as a prophet. His story grips us so tightly that it enables us to see more clearly our own lives through the eyes of God.

Proposition: Seeing our lives through God's eyes can motivate us to greater devotion and obedience.

I. OUR RELIGIOUS DEVOTION TO GOD NEEDS TO BE TOTAL.

A. Everyone here probably recognizes temporary lapses in religious practice in their own lives. You know you should be more attentive to God's things. You should attend worship more often. You should catch up on your tithe. You should assume some responsibility within the church. You should visit the sick in the name of Christ. You should, you should, you tell yourself. Then you tell yourself that one day you will—when that next project at work is behind you, when soccer season is over, when Christmas shopping is done, when, when, when, the byword of wishful thinking.

B. But in the story of Hosea and Gomer we see this devotion through God's eyes. What we see as a slight lapse, God calls fornication. What? Fornication? "But I have not run off to other gods," you protest. "I have not been unfaithful by denying Christ," you declare. "I am not a spiritual prostitute."

Never mind that. Just as surely as denial of complete loyalty and devotion to Hosea makes Gomer unfaithful, our denial of complete loyalty and devotion to God makes us unfaithful. Fornication began before Gomer committed the act of betrayal. Her sin began when she desired other men. The completion of the act was just that, the completion, but her unfaithfulness to Hosea began much earlier. When we deny complete loyalty and devotion to God, we have committed spiritual adultery as surely as Gomer committed physical adultery.

C. If my wife came home only occasionally, thumbed through the personal ads in search of a man to her liking, frequented singles bars, and spent hours on the phone talking to her single friend about the men they had met, even if she had not yet left me for another man, I would feel heartbroken, betrayed, and distraught.

    If we worship and pray only occasionally, yet thumb through the catalogs in search of things on which to spend our tithe, spend our spare time watching R-rated movies and listening to less than uplifting music, and spend hours talking to our friends about our latest material conquests, even while we still claim to be Christian, God feels heartbroken, betrayed, and distraught.

II. OUR DAILY BEHAVIOR MUST DRAW OTHERS TO GOD.

A. As far as you are concerned, your behavior may be your business and may affect only you. You know it is wrong, but you will straighten it out later. Nothing could be further from the truth.

B. The children born to Hosea and Gomer reveal the fallacy of such thinking. Each child was given a prophetic name—Jezreel ("I will soon punish"), Lo-Ruhamah ("Not loved"), and Lo-Ammi ("Not my people")—to teach Israel that the second generation would be burdened by their parents' denial of loyalty and devotion (Hosea 1:4-9).

C. All too often I have seen parents busy themselves with jobs, recreational pursuits, or educational interests, always putting those things ahead of their devotion to God. All the while their children are growing up. Then, one day the parents decide to get serious about their faith. By then their nearly grown children say, "Not me! I'm not interested in that religious stuff." I have seen near middle-age adults coming back to the church, sitting with their sulking, sullen, teenage children who don't understand what this sudden Christian urge is all about. In many ways children carry the names or the results of the parents' lack of loyalty and devotion. Through the eyes of Hosea and Gomer we see this behavior through God's eyes.

D. It is as if God says, "If you won't listen to me, if you won't be loyal and devoted for your own reasons, listen to your children. Be loyal for their sake!"

CONCLUSION

    Hear God say, "Please see your life as I see it. If you want to know the reality of our relationship, imagine that you have an unfaithful spouse and that your kids are children of unfaithful parents."

    When there is unfaithfulness within a marriage, the behavior of the unfaithful partner proclaims, "I have no love for you, kids. I must have what I want first" or "You're not my people. You can have what is left of me after I get what I want." And when there is unfaithfulness in our marriage to God, we are saying to God and to our children, "You are not mine."

The Nature of Repentance

Joel 1:14; 2:12-14

Junior highers invest great time and effort trying to work out their social order. Perhaps you've seen a group of them flitting around at a school event, trying to find out if they can get one boy and one girl together without either risking rejection.

The game continues into adulthood, but the stakes are much higher. Some of the same dynamics can be observed with important issues such as sin, repentance, and forgiveness. "I'll say I'm sorry when he says he's sorry" or "I'll admit I was wrong when he admits he was wrong too." Pride keeps us from volunteering a confession or asking for forgiveness without some indication that it will be graciously accepted and reciprocated. Who is going to make the first move? Will I lose face?

Reflecting on these dynamics of human relationships helps us think about the message of the book of Joel. To do so we move from relationships between people to relationships between people and God.

Joel 2:12-14 forms a transition from a description of a present disaster (1:2-20) and the threat of a worse future disaster (2:1-11) to an offer of grace to those who repent. In the process, God, through the prophet Joel, gives some valuable insights into the dynamics of repentance.

Proposition: All people, both non-Christians and Christians alike, need to repent.

I. THE SAME LORD WHO SENDS LOCUSTS INVITES REPENTANCE (1:14; 2:12).

A. After announcing the Lord's involvement in the swarms of locusts that came on the sinful nation of Judah, Joel instructed the people, "Declare a holy fast; call a sacred assembly" (1:14). Such a solemn assembly was for the purpose of corporate repentance. Only the repentant prayer of God's people would bring healing to the land.

B. I have participated in small-group prayer, congregational, and community-wide prayer meetings. However, I have yet to see a community, congregation, or small group call a prayer meeting for the purpose of repenting before God as a corporate act.

C. Perhaps the response to the dangers on our streets today should be repentance rather than more police. This repentance should be by the "good" people who are not committing the crimes but who have forgotten God, by the religious people who are simply going through the motions.

II. REPENTANCE ALWAYS HAS A SENSE OF URGENCY TO IT (2:12)

A. Sin always brings estrangement. To live life in estrangement from God, day after day and year after year, is not only harmful for the present but dangerous for one's future prospects. The matter is urgent.

B. In Mark 1:15, Jesus reiterates the urgency of repentance: "The time has come. The kingdom of God is near. Repent, and believe the good news." John the Baptist speaks with similar urgency: "Repent, for the kingdom of heaven is near" (Matthew 3:2). Repentance must not be delayed whether it is a time of national suffering or a time of God's clear action to save. In either case, God calls for a repentance seen in rending of hearts and not of garments (Joel 2:13).

C. Even without the threat of doom, the very nature of repentance carries with it an urgency, the urgency of making things right with another.

III. GOD REMAINS SOVEREIGN EVEN IN THE FACE OF REPENTANCE (2:14).

A. The last half of verse 13 and the first part of 14 teach that, perhaps, because of God's forgiving nature, he will repent of the punishment he has planned. The decision whether or not to withdraw the punishment remains his. He is not bound by the repentance of Israel to withdraw the punishment.

B. In 1998 there was a famous case of execution for murder. Carla had committed horribly gruesome murders but became a Christian during her time on death row. Many thought her genuine repentance should earn her a pardon from the punishment. But Hebrews 12:17 says of Esau that he "could bring about no change of mind, though he sought the blessing with tears." Repentance is not just being sorry. People can be sorry and yet have no opportunity to undo the consequences of their sinful behavior. That remains in the hands of our sovereign God.

CONCLUSION

I am disturbed when parents teach their children to say "I'm sorry" but impose no punishment or consequences for the wrong behavior that elicited the need to say "I'm sorry." In so doing, we teach children that the words are enough and that the wronged person is bound to forgive once they are spoken. This is not true with humans, and it is not true with God. Although God invites us to repent and even sends punishment to motivate us to repent, he never promises that we will avoid the consequences of our sinful actions. Christians and non-Christians alike should heed God's urgent call to repent simply because they want to restore their broken relationship with God, with no thought that doing so will somehow deliver them from the repercussions of their own sin.

A Jealous God?

Joel 2:18-20

I've always been fascinated by the idea of a jealous God. Jealousy has always been seen as a negative idea by me. Even though I felt plenty of jealousy during the early years of my interest in girls, I knew even then that it was not a positive trait.

On many occasions I have counseled couples getting married about jealousy, and I have often helped already-married couples overcome jealous behavior. Yet God's Word insists that he is a jealous God. In Joel 2:18, God's jealousy for his land is connected with pity for his people. It is part of his response to their repentance. Even though human repentance does not obligate a sovereign God to forgive, God's jealousy causes him to respond positively to forgive.

What, then, does this jealousy of God mean? What do we make of this? Is this the same kind of jealousy we experience? If so, how can God experience such a base characteristic? Or if God's jealousy causes him to forgive a repentant people, perhaps this trait in God is not the same as the trait we call jealousy in ourselves. Joel 2:18-20 helps us discover the answers to these questions.

Proposition: Our jealous God longs for us to return to him so he can forgive us.

I. PERHAPS GOD'S JEALOUSY IS A CONSUMING FIRE FOR THOSE HE LOVES.

A. Leonard Coppes writes that there are three basic uses of the root word for jealousy: "a purely descriptive sense to denote one of the characteristics of living men (Eccl 9:6), or in a derogatory sense to denote hostile and disruptive passions (Prov 27:4) or in a favorable sense to denote consuming zeal focused on one that is loved (Ps 69:9 [H10])" *(Theological Wordbook of the Old Testament,* 2:802).

B. So perhaps God's jealousy is simply a consuming zeal focused on one that he loves! The words "consuming zeal" and "love" give this a much better ring, and I begin to become more comfortable with the idea of God being a jealous God. Still, something bothers me about this. When I think about my own experience of jealousy, there is a strange discomfort attached to the idea that God's jealousy is just a consuming zeal focused on those he loves. If this is what jealousy really is, why did I feel more passionate jealousy when I was dating than when I really came to love the woman to whom I'm married?

It isn't that I think God's jealousy and mine must be the same. It is simply that my experience of jealousy is what I have to go on for my understanding of this emotion. I don't automatically separate God's jealousy and mine. So we must define this word more carefully.

II. MORE SPECIFICALLY, GOD IS JEALOUS FOR THAT WHICH IS TRULY HIS.

A. Coppes also notes, "This verb expresses a very strong emotion whereby some quality or possession of the object is desired by the subject." The same root word denotes both "envy" and "jealousy." Envy is zeal for another's property. Jealousy is zeal for one's own property. Therefore, if I desire something that is yours, I am envious. If I desire something of mine that is in your possession, or if I don't want it to come into your possession, I experience jealousy.

B. This goes beyond the idea of God being jealous for his people because he loves them. God desires his people because he loves them and because they are his. But does this elevate God's jealousy above that which we experience, or does it bring him down to our level? To think of God in connection with the word "jealous" seems to bring him down to our level, and that makes many of us uncomfortable.

C. How is God's jealousy different from jealousy in mortals? Since jealousy is most commonly seen in male/female relationships, it is most helpful to compare God's relationship to his people with the marriage relationship.

III. GOD JEALOUSLY DESIRES FOR HIS PEOPLE TO BE LOYAL TO HIM.

A. Since God is Israel's husband, idolatry is depicted as spiritual adultery, and God responds to this adultery with a jealous desire for restored loyalty and devotion.

B. In light of all we have considered, we can arrive at the following conclusions:
1. Envy is desire or zeal for that which belongs to another.
2. Jealousy is desire or zeal for that which you love and belongs to you.
3. Jealousy is triggered by unfaithfulness of the one owned and loved. (In a marriage, the two partners become one and thus own one another.)
4. Jealousy causes one to forgive because jealousy wants the loved and owned one back. While God is sovereign and our repentance does not obligate him to forgive, he does forgive us when we repent. Indeed, he invites our repentance—because he is a jealous God.

CONCLUSION:

According to Joel 2:17, 18, the repentant prayer of the priests leads a jealous God to relieve the suffering of the repentant people. It is this quality in God that assures us of the ends to which he will go to bring us to himself when we are repentant.

The Tapestry of Life

Amos

One of my favorite ways of viewing many passages of Scripture is borrowed from Andrew Blackwood, a great preacher of the past. He would often speak of the "warp" and "woof" of the passage. These words are borrowed from the craft of weaving. The warp is the foundational thread put on the loom first. It determines the dimensions and strength of the tapestry. The woof is the thread woven back and forth through the warp to complete the cloth and make the pattern.

An overview of the prophecy of Amos reveals a beautiful tapestry of thought and interaction with God. Amos speaks of timeless principles that speak of God's relationship to physical creation and to mankind. Woven through the warp of these principles are various behaviors of God's people, Israel. Viewing the word pictures Amos paints makes it evident that some behaviors form a beautiful tapestry, while others clash so heavily with the colors of the warp that the tapestry will be ruined.

Proposition: Our lives interact with God's truth to create a beautiful tapestry or an ugly piece to be destroyed.

I. GOD'S PRINCIPLES SHOULD MAKE UP THE WARP OF OUR LIVES.

A. God speaks powerful truths to his people. Amos 4:13, for example, states that the Lord "forms the mountains, creates the wind, and reveals his thoughts to man." Note also that the phrase "This is what the Lord says" introduces every paragraph from 1:3 through 2:6. Moreover, when God speaks, his words carry great weight. Amos 1:2 says, "The Lord roars . . . and the top of Carmel withers." Likewise, 3:8 declares, "The lion has roared—who will not fear?"

B. God will ultimately oversee justice and righteousness. Amos 5:7 warns those "who turn justice into bitterness and cast righteousness to the ground" that God will punish them for their sins. God also exhorts, "Let justice roll on like a river, righteousness like a never-failing stream" (5:24).

C. Since God will judge all people according to his revealed will, it is worthwhile to note what God loves and hates. In 5:15 Amos tells us, "Hate evil, love good; maintain justice in the courts." If we fail to do this, God will say to us, as he did to the people of Amos's day, "I hate, I despise your religious feasts; I cannot stand your assemblies" (5:21). "I abhor the pride of Jacob and detest his fortresses" (6:8).

These three principles, then, form the warp of our lives: 1) God speaks to his people. 2) God will oversee justice, righteousness, and judgment. 3) God will speak and judge based on his hatred of evil and love of good.

II. OUR BEHAVIOR FORMS THE WOOF OF OUR LIVES, FOR GOOD OR EVIL.

A. The people of that day said they looked forward to the day of the Lord even though they did not live as they should have. They felt secure in their cities and their religion (5:21-23) as well as in their prosperity (6:4-6). A smug sense of security rising out of religious formalism and material comfort does not fit well as the woof in a tapestry, the warp of which is made up of the revelation of a sovereign God who makes clear his justice, righteousness, and goodness. For such people, the day of the Lord would be doom (5:18).

B. The same is true today. People today define truth to fit their behavior. We are told, "People will sin anyway, so let's help them to sin safely." Only, we don't say "sin." We say "choice," "behavior," or some other neutral word. We no longer look for a sovereign source of truth. Rather, we define it for ourselves.

C. Interest in religion is on the increase. Great churches are being built and filled with worshipers. At the same time, there is an increasing interest in angels, ghosts, and spirits. Traditional Christian faith is being replaced by faith shaped by postmodernism, which believes that all truth is relative.

D. Finally, a recent full page ad in a major newspaper urges us to buy a particular car and "excite our souls." Materialism is rampant to the extent that devout Christians struggle with how much to own and indifferent churches arrange service times so worshipers can get to the local restaurant for Sunday lunch ahead of people from a neighboring church. All these signs indicate that the woof of our lives does not fit the warp of God's truth.

CONCLUSION

We could go on and on with the characteristics of our day. The more we compare today to Israel in the days of Amos, the more frightening it becomes. We need to cry out for repentance in the land. Our tapestry is not good! The colors clash! Then we must begin in our homes, our churches, and our communities to weave new cloth. We must weave acts of justice, love, and righteousness with the truths of God's Word about loving that which is good and hating that which is evil.

The God of Amos

Amos 1:3–2:3; 4:13; 5:4-6

During Jesus' ministry, many disbelieved and tested him. Once, in a response to the testing of the Sadducees, he said, "You are in error because you do not know the Scriptures or the power of God" (Matthew 22:29). Jesus did not debate the issue of resurrection with them but pointed them to the Word of God and the power of God.

Today people are unsure about who God is. Some imagine there is a god within each person, while others believe in a Mother Earth god. Ours is a pluralist society, and the prevailing spirit of tolerance demands that we accept any definition of God without dissent, no matter what someone might believe.

The prophet Amos faced similar circumstances. Long before his time there were periods during which Israel assimilated worship practices of the Canaanite gods into their worship of the true god. They considered themselves to be faithful followers of God, but Amos felt the need to reinforce their knowledge of God's characteristics. As he preached God's message of displeasure with their behavior, they were reminded of who this God was.

Proposition: Our God is the God of creation, the nations, and salvation!

I. THE GOD OF THE BIBLE IS THE GOD OF CREATION (4:13).

A. Amos 4:13 declares, "He who forms the mountains, creates the wind . . . who turns dawn to darkness, and treads the high places of the earth—the Lord God Almighty is his name." For Christians, belief in God's creation of all there is goes without saying, but for non-Christians it cannot be assumed. Moreover, although the people of Amos's day would have agreed to this, they did not act as though they understood the implications of worshiping the creator God.

B. One implication of God being creator is that he controls the physical universe. Jesus, in whom dwelt all the fullness of deity bodily (Colossians 2:9), exhibited this power in his ministry through such miracles as stilling the storm. The point is that the maker of something has authority to determine its purpose, its duration, and its disposal. Think about things you have made, and see if you do not feel this way about them. Or think about a five-year-old bringing you a picture she has drawn. She will tell you what it is, where to put it, and when you can or cannot dispose of it. At that tender age we know that the one who creates is in control of that which is created.

C. It is good stewardship to care for our planet, but we must not go to the extreme of thinking that the planet's destiny depends on us. This is God's planet. Even the Pleiades and Orion are his (5:8, 9). We are stewards, privileged to live here for a while.

II. THE GOD OF THE BIBLE IS THE GOD OF THE NATIONS (1:3–2:3).

A. The creator God is not just the God of Israel and Judah. According to Amos, he is not merely the God of Abraham, Isaac, and Jacob. Nations of that day were accustomed to thinking of gods in such terms. Israel had its God, while Edom, Ammon, and Moab had theirs.

B. Amos demolishes that perspective by holding all nations accountable to the one true God. All nations will answer to the creator God whether or not they acknowledge him. God will stand in judgment of those whom he has given life. He does not need the assent of a nation before he can judge it.

C. People today seem to think they can determine their own national destinies by legislating and limiting God's place in society. But the fact is, nothing people do, either on their own or through political processes, will alter God's power to control both their individual and national destinies.

III. THE GOD OF THE BIBLE IS THE GOD OF SALVATION (5:4-6).

A. While it is tempting to read Amos with an emphasis on judgment, the other side of judgment is atonement.

B. The people of Amos's day looked forward to the day of the Lord because they imagined that their well-polished religion would place them in good stead in God's presence. However, they were told in 5:18-20 not to look forward to the day of the Lord because God hated their religious offerings.

C. "Seek me and live" is the cry of a caring God even in the darkest hours. The God who is powerful enough to save has a heart that desires to save. Amidst all of Amos's warnings, it is easy to miss this twice-repeated plea (5:4, 6). The reason the day of the Lord would not be a blessing for Israel was not because God looked forward to punishing them. Rather, the people refused to let him be the God of their salvation through acquittal. They hoped to gain salvation by a formal nod in God's direction, but that does not constitute surrender to a sovereign God.

CONCLUSION

Almost eight hundred years after Amos, Jesus spoke the Great Commission. It is the commission to make disciples, a commission to save. Note that even the Great Commission begins with "authority." It is because of the sovereign authority of God who is Lord that we have hope and purpose today.

Revelation and the Need to Proclaim

Amos 4:13

Donald G. Bloesch, in *God the Almighty: Power, Wisdom, Holiness, Love,* quotes Eberhard Jungel as saying, "Against both mystical and scholastic theology I maintain that we cannot reach God by the way of virtue of thought but God can come to us and enable us to think what was previously unthinkable." Bloesch adds, "Jungel makes a telling point that in philosophy thought is prior to speech, but in biblical Christianity speech is prior to thought. We know as we are addressed" (p. 61).

This is a fancy way of saying that we cannot think up our religion, that it must be revealed to us by a sovereign God. Likewise, Arthur Leff, former law professor at Harvard, struggled to decide what is finally right and just. Eventually he recognized that without the "unevaluated evaluator" to tell us what is finally right and just we are doomed. Leff closed his 1979 lecture at Duke University with these words:

> Neither reason, nor love, nor even terror, seems to have worked to make us "good," and worse than that, there is no reason why anything should. . . . As things stand now, everything is up for grabs.
>
> Nevertheless: Napalming babies is bad. Starving the poor is wicked. Buying and selling each other is depraved. Those who stood up and died resisting Hitler, Stalin, Amin, and Pol Pot—and General Custer too—have earned salvation. Those who acquiesced deserve to be damned. There is in the world such a thing as evil. God help us.

So speaks the heart of an intelligent philosopher of law crying out to believe that God has told us what is right and wrong. Amos 4:13 has the answer: "He who forms the mountains, creates the wind, and reveals his thoughts to man, he who turns dawn to darkness, and treads the high places of the earth—the Lord God Almighty is his name."

**Proposition: Since God has given us the truth,
we must accept and speak his truth to everyone around us.**

I. GOD HAS TOLD US WHAT HE THINKS, SO WE MUST ACCEPT HIS WORD AS TRUTH.

A. Philosophers have struggled for centuries to arrive at "truth." Pontius Pilate passed off Jesus by asking, "What is truth?" then didn't stay around for the answer. Today people govern their lives by a philosophy called relativism. In it there is no absolute truth; truth is whatever an individual perceives it to be. Allan Bloom notes, "There is one thing a professor can be absolutely certain of: almost every student entering the university believes, or says he believes, that truth is relative" *(The Closing of the American Mind,* 25)

B. Amos faced the same problem. He wrote, "You hate the one who reproves in court and despise him who tells the truth" (5:10).

C. According to the Bible, we can know the truth because it has been revealed by the one who ultimately is truth. Philosophers have spent their lives in quest of truth, but the fact of the matter is that we must be told the truth by the one who, by speaking it, makes it truth.

II. GOD *IS* THE TRUTH, SO WE MUST ACCEPT AND SPEAK HIS WORD AS TRUTH.

A. When God speaks, nature responds—"the top of Carmel withers" (Amos 1:2). There is also an expected response by humans: responsibility. God explains in Amos 3:2: "You only have I chosen of all the families of the earth; therefore I will punish you for all your sins."

B. Amos also presents the case in terms of natural cause and effect, namely, that when God speaks, we should speak, "The lion has roared—who will not fear? The Sovereign Lord has spoken—who can but prophesy?" (3:8).

III. IF WE FAIL TO TELL GOD'S TRUTH, WE WILL SUFFER ITS LOSS IN OUR LIVES.

A. According to Amos 8:11-14, God threatened to send a famine of his word, and people would stop hearing what God thinks. Such a time in which the well of God's revelation was dried up would be a time for perishing. Those who can't hear a word from the Lord will stumble through lives of utter despair. In the absence of God's Word, being young and bright and vigorous will not help. There is no place to go, no one to talk to, no thought to think that will take the place of knowing the truth that is God and that is told by God.

B. Throughout history every attempt by humans to deny the creator God and to arrive at our own philosophy that will enlighten and give meaning to life has ended in despair.

CONCLUSION

We already know the truth because God has told us! We know the truth because we have met the One who is the Way, the Truth, and the Life! It is imperative that we proclaim it with ever growing intensity to our churches, to our neighbors, to our co-workers. And before they can hear what we say, it is necessary for them to see us living the truth that we will tell them.

Seeing God in Our World

Amos 4:6-12

Some people claim God helps them find parking spaces at the mall, while others believe that he helps their team to win an important game. I don't know. Does God care who wins the Super Bowl?

On the other hand, I also see people face serious hardships without ever looking for God in them. Floods, droughts, hurricanes, earthquakes—is God in them? If we say he is not in them, we risk learning nothing from them. If we say he is in them, we have the job of figuring out what it is he wants us to learn from them.

The prophets interpreted events to help people know just how, why, and when God was in such natural events. Amos does so for the people of Israel. Life was good for them, and in their prosperity they had a tendency to miss seeing God in natural calamities or political catastrophes.

Proposition: God uses natural events to call people and nations back to him and to prepare them to meet him.

I. AMOS SAW GOD CALLING PEOPLE BACK TO HIM IN SUCH EVENTS.

A. Amos 4:6-11 lists various things God had done to Israel:

1. He gave them empty stomachs in every city (v. 6).
2. He withheld the rain when harvest was three months away (v. 7).
3. He laid waste gardens, vineyards, fig trees, and olive trees (v. 9).
4. He sent pestilence and killed their young men with the sword (v. 10).
5. He overthrew some of them as he had overthrown Sodom and Gomorrah (v. 11).

B. In each case, Amos notes, "'you have not returned to me,' declares the Lord" (4:6, 8, 9, 10, 11). Obviously, it was God's intent for these events to cause his people to return to him. But the people of Israel had been so busy with their own prosperity, political security, and religious practices that it did not occur to them that God was trying to get their attention. They were self-sufficient, they thought, and generally life was very good.

C. God had made a covenant with Israel that dated back to Abraham. They had broken the covenant by treating their worship as an idol. Even though they continued to go through the motions of worshiping God, their worship was not acceptable. They were guilty of formalism.

God's covenant with us today is different. It is a covenant of grace and is made with the church rather than with a nation. However, there is still something to consider. If we believe in God's immanence, we must be conscious of the possibility that God will intervene in world events to get his people to return to him. The repentance of people who are God's people, and the repentance of the nations in which they live, is still valid. The church should issue the call to repentance for the world around it. This is the call to salvation.

II. AMOS SAW SUCH EVENTS AS PRECURSORS TO MEETING GOD.

A. Whether or not you and I can correctly identify the events that are especially brought about by God for a specific purpose, there is something that is certain. Sooner or later we will all be called to account.

In the movie *Princess Bride,* there is a character who roams the world hoping to avenge his father's murder. When he meets a stranger who might have been the murderer, he introduces himself, tells the stranger of his suspicions that he may have killed his father, then tells the stranger to prepare to die. He is going to see to it that the villain is called to account for his act.

B. Amos is just as sure that all people will meet God. All people will eventually meet their maker. In light of this truth, it becomes less important for any one person to identify a particular event, be it flood, earthquake, or drought, as a specific act to call a specific people to repentance. Rather, the universal truth about meeting our God bears within it a universal call to preparation for that meeting. Every experience of a powerful event that holds the potential to take life from us should remind us again of the frailty of our lives. This refreshed realization should call us, at that moment, to "return to" him.

C. If we should, as believers, recognize this, it still does not extend to our nation, for God has not made a covenant with any nation today as he did with Israel. How do we call our nation to the realization that it, too, will meet its Creator? This must be done person by person until there is in the land a majority of sincere, humble, practicing Christians. Then, and only then, will the nation be able to hear Amos's call to repentance. Either way, the plight of our nation is the same as for a covenant nation. It will meet its God.

CONCLUSION

This becomes, then, a sermon urging evangelism. Obedient faith in Jesus Christ is the only thing that will save an individual or a nation. The more God's people concentrate on doing his business and the more sincerely their hearts open to him to reach out to unbelievers, the more likely God is to look with favor on the nation. His patience had run out with Israel. We dare not let his patience run out with us.

Acceptable Worship

Amos 5:18-24

What constitutes good worship? Isn't that the question today? Too often we hear of churches dividing over worship styles. People decide where they will attend based on the kinds of musical instruments or the types of songs used in worship.

In today's narcissistic society, we have the impression that the acceptability of worship is determined by the way we feel. If there isn't something that "moves us," we just can't worship. "Those old hymns are so boring." "Those new songs are so loud." "The words in those old hymns are so strange. I don't know what half of them mean." "They just sing those choruses over and over, and they stand up so long while they sing them."

On and on it goes. People polarize along the lines of their favorite worship style. This is what Joe Ellis in his book, *The Church on Purpose*, refers to as a "solidary" incentive for being in church. It has more to do with the worshiper than with God. So what is the type of worship that pleases God?

**Proposition: God honors worship focused on him
and offered by people obedient to him.**

I. ACCEPTABLE WORSHIP FOCUSES ON GOD, NOT THE WORSHIPER.

A. The Israelites had two clear problems that destroyed the effectiveness of their worship. The first is that they sought to please themselves instead of God in their worship. The people of Amos's day loved their religious festivals and traditions, the offering of sacrifices and the singing of songs. Eventually they grew so enamored with the trappings of worship that they forgot its purpose, to honor God.

B. Today people openly look for a church with worship that meets their needs. Some churches even use worship as a means of reaching the lost. Certainly this deserves serious thought. What is the point of having worship services in empty buildings? Why not use worship to draw people to the Lord?

C. But there is something uncomfortable about that for me. I don't find the Bible encouraging us to use worship to draw people to God. Rather, worship is something that takes place among believers. While the synagogues of New

Testament times welcomed the "devout" Gentiles, that was not the primary purpose of the synagogue worship, and the services were not designed for the Gentiles.

D. If the quality of worship is not determined by the way it moves the worshipers or its success in drawing the unchurched, how do we determine its quality? While Amos is by no means the only Scripture writer to address the subject, he does offer some serious things to think about. God was clearly not pleased with the worship of the Israelites when Amos prophesied, and he has plenty to say about it (5:18-24).

E. Up to this point we have concerned ourselves only with what affects people in worship. People have been the focus. But what does God think of worship? We have to consider not only what God thinks about our worship but also whether our worship is primarily for us or for God. Amos's main concern is whether worship is acceptable to God—not whether it helps, pleases, fulfills, or lifts the worshipers.

F. Comments such as "hate," "despise," "cannot stand," "will not accept," "will have no regard for," and "will not listen" convey the prophet's (and God's) perspective on Israel's worship. This has an immediate impact on us. What if today, as then, God hates the worship we love? Is that possible? Why should we be different from them in this respect? If we are designing worship to feel good to us, why can we not be as wrong as they were?

II. ACCEPTABLE WORSHIP CAN ONLY BE OFFERED BY AN OBEDIENT PEOPLE.

A. God was not displeased with the style of the Israelites' worship. Rather, God was displeased with their worship because it was not offered to him by just and righteous people (Amos 5:23, 24).

B. Herein lies the crux of the matter. Just and righteous people do not focus on worship styles or their own worship needs. Rather, they come before God as humble and obedient humans who want only to worship God through their prayers, songs, and very lives. Instead of concerning ourselves with styles of worship, we should focus our attention on God, on pleasing him both with our acts of worship and our daily acts of obedience.

CONCLUSION

The divisiveness that causes many of us to separate over worship style suggests that we may have our own shortcomings in justice and righteousness. In fact, this divisiveness may make our worship unacceptable to God regardless of its style! If we divide, even in heart or mind, over a worship style, we should tremble before God, repent, and come together in love, justice, and righteousness to worship him. This, regardless of style, will be good worship.

Good and Evil

Amos and Habakkuk

The God who is sovereign and who has told us what he thinks is the one who defines good and evil. Granted, humans are given consciences to tell us to do good and to avoid evil. However, those consciences are trained, whether for good or for evil. Indeed, we are training our children's consciences when we teach them right from wrong.

For example, because I was taught the sanctity of other people's property as a child, I cannot use an envelope from my office for personal business without my conscience telling me this is wrong. Another person raised by parents who regularly brought home items from their workplaces might use company stationery with no pangs of conscience at all.

In an age of relativism, many people behave in sinful ways without any pangs of conscience. Because of this, people without an authoritative guide for defining good and evil find themselves either in conflict over what they have defined as good and evil or in the despair of believing that there is no one with enough moral authority to give anything meaning. But the sovereign God has told us what he thinks, so we should listen carefully to what he has said.

> **Proposition: God's people must hate evil and love good
> as God has defined the evil and the good.**

I. WE MUST UNDERSTAND WHAT GOD THINKS ABOUT GOOD AND EVIL.

A. God's involvement in human affairs defines good and evil. He determines truth, and he will determine the truth about whether something is good or evil. Think of Joseph's comment to his brothers concerning their selling him to the slave traders: "You intended to harm me, but God intended it for good to accomplish what is now being done, the saving of many lives" (Genesis 50:20).

B. This perspective is also present in Amos and Habakkuk. Amos asks, "When a trumpet sounds in a city, do not the people tremble? When disaster comes to a city, has not the Lord caused it?" (Amos 3:6). Later he adds, "Though they are driven into exile by their enemies, there I will command the sword to slay them. I will fix my eyes upon them for evil and not for good" (9:4).

C. Habakkuk, on the other hand, wanted to define good and evil for God. He complained to God about evil Judah and asked God to do something about it. When God told him that he would use the "evil" Babylonians to take Judah captive, Habakkuk was shocked (1:12). He wanted to define good and evil for God and tell God what he should do about both. However, God had reserved that prerogative for himself.

D. Part of recognizing God's sovereignty is accepting that it is God who defines good and evil. It is also recognizing that, when we are his people, we must commit to loving what he calls good and hating what he calls evil—even in our personal behavior. To fail to do so causes us to be in danger of sinning in our personal behavior and being hypocritical in our judgment of others. It also diminishes our ability to recognize God's presence in the nations of the world.

II. WE MUST ALSO ADOPT GOD'S PERSPECTIVE ON GOOD AND EVIL.

A. Amos said of Israel, "You hate the one who reproves in court and despise him who tells the truth" (5:10). Israel has lost sight of God's priorities. This is why Israel committed the atrocities Amos lists even while they claimed to be God's people.

In the same way, a materialistic people will not be very concerned with truth, especially as it relates to good and evil. Whatever gives them more material things will be truth enough for them.

B. But the presence of God with us is contingent on our attitude toward good and evil. We are told both to seek and to love good. The consequence of doing this is not only that we will live but that the Lord will also be with us (Amos 5:14). This is as true for nations as for individuals. A people who want to reject the truth God has told them in favor of a truth they invent have already despised or hated God. When they need him, he will not be there because he has been despised.

C. Therefore, it is important not only to understand what God thinks about good and evil but to love good and hate evil. Willpower is not enough for doing good. It will be much easier for me to be honest when I love honesty and hate dishonesty.

CONCLUSION

God commands us to love good and hate evil and to recognize that we are not empowered to define either. Neither community standards nor the opinions of the well-intentioned are adequate for defining good and evil. Therefore, we must think of and live by God's definition of the issue.

Loving What God Loves

Amos 5:14, 15, 21-24

"I hate anchovies on pizza."
"I hate bluegrass music."
"I hate it when I sleep in a bad position and wake up stiff and sore."
"I hate it when students cut classes then make up lame excuses."
"I love strawberry rhubarb pie."
"I love blonde hair and blue eyes."
"I love baroque music."
"I love the mountains."

What do hate and love mean in this context? We all use the words this way. We know we aren't talking about the same depth of emotion as when we say, "I love my wife" or "I hate what cancer does to one's body."

In the Old Testament, as today, the words "love" and "hate" were used both for abstract and concrete things. For example, God loves his people (concrete) but hates evil (abstract).

Amos spoke powerfully about God's revelation, his speaking to humanity: "The Lord roars from Zion and thunders from Jerusalem; the pastures of the shepherds dry up, and the top of Carmel withers" (1:2). Later on, Amos writes, "The lion has roared—who will not fear?" (3:8). This same revelation told, in numerous places in Amos, of God's scorn for the injustice and materialism of Israel. There he exhorted Israel, "Seek good, not evil" (5:14) and "Hate evil, love good" (5:15). All that seems simple enough, doesn't it?

But what does it mean to hate evil as God does, to love good as God loves good? If we would learn the lesson of Amos for our day, we must learn to measure all our decisions according to their fit or clash with God's revelation of eternal principles regarding good and evil.

Proposition: We must learn to love what God loves and hate what he hates.

I. THOSE WHO LOVE WHAT GOD HATES DO NOT LOVE GOD OR WHAT HE LOVES.

    A. According to Amos 6:4-6, the Israelites loved their material possessions too much. They loved their fine houses, rich food, entertainment, and leisure. They were too busy with these to grieve over the loss of principle and justice in the land.

B. On the other hand, the people hated the poor and needy—not injustice (8:4-6). They thoughtlessly bought and sold the poor and needy by cheating them in business, if not in outright indentured servitude. They were accused of loving injustice and hating justice. Thus Amos writes in 5:10, "You hate the one who reproves in court and despise him who tells the truth."

C. It may not always be a question of what you hate but of what you love. When I love the wrong things too much, it automatically causes me to hate the right things. No one can serve God and Money, Jesus reminds us. "Either he will hate the one and love the other, or he will be devoted to the one and despise the other" (Matthew 6:24). In other words, if we love what God hates, we do not love what he loves. It's one or the other. We can't have it both ways.

II. GOD LOVES THE WORSHIP OF ONLY THOSE WHO LOVE WHAT HE LOVES.

A. The people of Amos's day hated justice and loved power, so God hated their worship. The people thought everything was going fine. They even looked forward to the day of the Lord because they were sure of their righteousness and of experiencing God's favor (Amos 5:18). Formalism is the consequence of people becoming so caught up in their own direction that they can't hear God any longer. They continue the forms of worship they love but without godliness. Needless to say, God hates and rejects such worship (5:21-23).

B. Consider Luke 6:6-9, the case of the healing of the man's withered hand on the Sabbath. When Jesus revealed the religious leaders' hypocritical religion, they began to plan what they might do to him. How could people who considered themselves righteous stoop to such depravity? They loved ceremony so much that they could not hear when God spoke. Consequently, they were able to plan and to do unthinkable things. They loved and hated the wrong things.

CONCLUSION

Weave your behavior, your deepest thoughts into the tapestry of God's Word. How does your life fit with God's truths? Do you love what he loves and hate what he hates? Many times when we have difficulty stopping a bad habit or developing a good attitude toward a certain person, it is because we love the wrong things. Like God, we must love good and hate evil.

A Discourse on Hatred

Obadiah

Many have heard of the Hatfields and McCoys, those feuding mountain people who hated each other long after a given generation knew how the hatred started. Others will recall the Capulets and Montagues, those feuding families from whom sprang the star-crossed lovers, Romeo and Juliet. And while most hatreds do not achieve the folk-lore status and color of these famous feuds, hatred continues to take its ugly toll on human beings in every age.

There is a rage, anger, or hatred evident in society today. It rears its ugly head each time there is an outbreak of violence in one of our schools or when an innocent child is shot by a drive-by gunman. This hatred forces us to build shelters for battered women and children and install metal detectors in many of our schools and in all of our airports. Emergency room physicians and nurses become experts in treating bullet and knife wounds because of this hatred.

What of this hatred? Obadiah is not going to tell us how to get rid of it. No, his message, properly understood, will tell us how to prevent anger from progressing to hatred. His message is more preventive than corrective because it presents a portrait of the extent to which hatred can carry us down the road to destruction, whether as individuals or as a nation.

It will help to recall the story behind the Edomites, those people against whom Obadiah pronounced God's judgment. They were descended from Esau, who sold his birthright to his brother Jacob for a single meal. The book of Hebrews calls Esau immoral because he prized the things of the body over things that were sacred. But this event triggered an anger on Esau's part that escalated into hatred, a hatred that would endure for countless years between the descendants of Jacob, the Jews, and the descendants of Esau, the Edomites.

We frequently think that hatred is excessive anger. I believe it is not so much the excess or heat of anger that creates hatred. Rather, I think it is the duration of angry habits that leads to hatred. Hatred occurs when the attributes of anger become a way of life.

Proposition: We must beware of letting the attributes of anger become a way of life.

I. HATEFUL THINKING CAUSES US TO MISUNDERSTAND WHO THE ENEMY IS.

A. We think our enemy is the people we hate. The Hatfields thought the enemy was the McCoys, while the Capulets thought it was the Montagues. Likewise, Edom thought Israel was "the enemy." When we hate, we fixate on the object of our hatred, thinking that one to be the enemy. This hatred is passed from generation to generation, long after the original reason for the anger has been forgotten. We "know" who the enemy is because he bears the name.

B. In reality, the hater's real enemy is God, as Obadiah implies: "I [God] will make you small among the nations. . . . I will bring you down." (vv. 2, 4). God cannot bless hatred. The God who is love stands for everything that hatred despises. Thus, because Edom has made God its enemy, he will bring them down.

II. HATEFUL THINKING CAUSES US TO OVERESTIMATE OUR OWN POWER.

A. Edom's stronghold, Petra, was located in a most defensible place. The city was carved into rock cliffs (vv. 3, 4), and the only entry into the city was gained by a narrow passageway between very high rock walls. An army would have to enter almost single file and would be easy to defeat from ambush. This caused Edom to think she was safe against all comers.

B. When we are angry or filled with hate, we often think ourselves to be stronger than we actually are. The often-heard expression, "Look out for me when I'm mad!" is an example of this overestimation of strength. In truth, we are often most vulnerable when angry. When people hate, they even imagine they can overcome God's rules for behavior.

III. HATEFUL THINKING LEADS US TO TAKE JOY AND PRIDE IN THE WRONG THINGS.

A. Edom had gloated, rejoiced, boasted, looted, and delivered up survivors when God's people suffered (vv. 12-14). They were actually glad to watch evil being done to the Israelites.

B. The Edomites held to the old "You'll get yours" mentality. Yet the same thing happens today. Once someone in a Bible study made the following prayer request: "A thief broke into my van last night and stole my radio. Will you pray that bad things happen to that person?" The desire for vengeance causes angry human beings to take pride and joy in things that others would grieve.

CONCLUSION

Obadiah ends by saying that "the kingdom will be the Lord's" (v. 21). Ultimately, God will have his way, and his way is not to bless your hatred. So if you have hatred in your life, do everything you can to get rid of it. Stop letting attributes of anger rule your life and lead you to hate. It is the ruin of the soul.

Controlling Your Temper

Jonah 4

Jonah may be the best known of the Minor Prophets. Even people who have not been in church may know the story of Jonah. Jonah will be remembered as the man who ran from God's instruction and ended up in the belly of a great fish for three days. But the part of the story that speaks most directly to the average person is not so well known. It is the part that deals with anger.

This is especially appropriate today because of the anger that is prevalent in our culture. Many crimes today are hate crimes—anger run amok. Homes are broken by continuous anger. Children grow up with anger as a daily reality. But God can help us, as he did Jonah, control our anger. [Tell the story of Jonah 4 in your own words.]

Proposition: We can learn to control our anger.

I. OUR ANGER IS MORE ABOUT US THAN ABOUT OTHERS.

A. What was Jonah angry about? Was he angry with the Ninevites? Was he angry with himself? No, he was angry with God because God forgave the repentant Ninevites. Jonah was angry with God because he did not want the Ninevites saved. Now we know his reason for fleeing to Tarshish in the first place. He did not regard the Ninevites highly enough to want them saved. To make matters worse, God had used him as an instrument in bringing about their salvation from destruction. That infuriated Jonah.

B. What about you? Do you sometimes get angry because bad people get good things or because people who deserve punishment aren't punished? It is not uncommon for a Christian wife to feel anger when her husband, who has mistreated her, becomes a Christian and changes. While others are rejoicing over his conversion, she is wondering why he should get off so easily. Why shouldn't he pay for the way he treated her? The first step in controlling our anger is recognizing that it is primarily about us, not others.

II. WE GET ANGRY ABOUT THE PEOPLE AND THINGS WE CARE ABOUT.

A. Jonah cared about the Hebrew heritage, about being God's own people, about being more in God's favor than other nations. These Assyrians didn't deserve God's favor, and now God was giving it to them. How dare God make them as important as the Israelites!

B. Note also how Jonah feels about the plant. It was useful to him for providing comfort. Jonah *cares* about the plant because it benefits him. So when Jonah becomes angry because the plant has died, he feels justified in his anger. It concerned, after all, something that he cared about.

C. Often we feel justified in the cause of our anger. Sometimes we feel justified in the fact of our anger. Have you ever heard someone say, "I don't get mad. I get even." This not only excuses anger but takes a certain pride in it. This kind of anger, the kind that Jonah felt, is based on pride and a self-serving attitude. The second step that will help us control our anger is asking ourselves if we should care about the cause of our anger as much as we do.

D. This would imply that all anger is not bad, that there is a kind of anger that is good. Since God made us with the ability to become angry, there must be a use for it. The New Testament says, "In your anger do not sin: Do not let the sun go down while you are still angry" (Ephesians 4:26). Jesus was angry with his disciples and with the money changers in the temple, so there must be some useful purpose for it.

III. THERE IS A TIME AND A PLACE FOR RIGHTEOUS INDIGNATION.

A. The key is in deciding what you care about. We will naturally become angry when the things we care about are violated. In effect, God says to Jonah, "You cared about the plant, not because you put yourself into it to grow or nurture it, but because it gave you comfort. Yet I have this city full of people to whom I gave life, for whom I care because of their value" (see 4:10, 11).

B. We can adjust our lives gradually as we grow to Christian maturity. We can adjust what we care about so that we care more about righteousness, justice, and salvation than about our own comfort and convenience. We get angry with the driver who cuts us off in traffic, not because we care so much about safety, but because we care about our time, our convenience, our space.

C. Rather, we should be like a friend of mine. When I stopped to see him at work one day, he was trembling with rage. He had been to McDonald's for lunch, where he saw a couple eating lunch in their car and frequently reaching into the back seat to hit a child who was crouching on the floor. He was enraged because he cared about the child's safety, so he immediately called the police. He got involved because of righteous indignation.

CONCLUSION

How do you use your anger—or does your anger use you? You can control your anger by controlling what you care about, and you can control what you care about by cultivating a correct view of your own importance as well as the importance of your possessions and space.

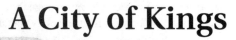

A City of Kings

Micah 5:2

Like Cinderella rising from the ashes and dust of the hearth, Bethlehem, a little town of no importance, rises to be the birthplace of kings. She is to be sung about for centuries to come. When the boundaries for Judah are set in Joshua 15 and the cities of Judah are named, Bethlehem is not considered significant enough to be included.

In Micah's day, the people were walled up in the city of Jerusalem, holding off Sennacherib's siege. Never had the remnant felt more alone, more helpless. Never had they seen less future for themselves. Never had the other nations been so sure of their fall (Micah 4:11). Judah's weakness is indicated by the fact that their king would suffer personal insult (Micah 5:1).

As I drive west on Interstate 70 in Kansas, I see large signs as I approach certain small towns. The signs give the town's name, then add, "home of . . ." and name an astronaut. People of these towns feel a connection with their famous and successful sons and daughters. It is not incidental that American presidents have come from insignificant towns made significant by the success of their sons. Such was also the case with Bethlehem.

> **Proposition: God uses insignificant places and people to accomplish significant deeds.**

I. BETHLEHEM WAS SIGNIFICANT BECAUSE OF GOD'S PRESENCE WITHIN IT.

A. There was nothing about the town of Bethlehem to make people great. It was not the seat of a great university or the home of fashion that it should set the standard for anything. It was given meaning by the people who came from it, and their greatness reflected back on it. Such is the case with Abilene, Kansas, Springfield, Illinois, and Independence, Missouri, the hometowns of Dwight Eisenhower, Abraham Lincoln, and Harry Truman respectively.

B. Bethlehem became extremely special because it is the place from which came the king, David, as well as the shoot "from the stump of Jesse" (Isaiah 11:1), Jesus the Messiah. In 1 Samuel 16:1 God told Samuel, "I am sending you to Jesse of Bethlehem. I have chosen one of his sons to be king." Centuries later God told Bethlehem, "Out of you will come for me one who will be ruler over Israel, whose origins are from of old, from ancient times" (Micah 5:2).

C. From the failed house of David, God goes back to the root of his father, Jesse, and raises up a king to keep the promise. It is not strange that the wise men went to Jerusalem looking for God's Messiah. Even today we take note when small towns produce great men and women. We expect great people to come from great settings, but with God, it is not so. God was in Bethlehem, and he chose that insignificant town to produce a king "for himself."

II. GOD USES THE LOWLY OF THE WORLD TO SHOW HIS GREAT POWER.

A. Not only does the choice of a lowly village fulfill prophecy and speak of God's working in these births, but it is also consistent with his choice of using the lowly to display his power. Whether by raising up a slave boy to embarrass Pharaoh or bringing a shepherd boy to the throne of his people, God always seems to work this way.

B. Paul states the principle for us in 1 Corinthians 1:18-31. In verse 25 he writes, "For the foolishness of God is wiser than man's wisdom, and the weakness of God is stronger than man's strength."

C. This village and these kings will be powerful because God has chosen them to be, not because of any human power or cleverness. One cannot think of these things without hearing God say in Isaiah, "neither are your ways my ways" (55:8)

III. GOD USES THE INSIGNIFICANT TO ACCOMPLISH SIGNIFICANT DEEDS.

A. Thousands make pilgrimages to Bethlehem each year. People want to see where it happened! Even with changes in worship music, we will likely continue to sing about Bethlehem. No matter what happens on this earth, no matter which nations rise and which fall, Bethlehem will remain a dearly loved place.

B. It reminds us that when God decides something will be great, it will be great. God wants us to be sure that we know our hope is not lost when we have setbacks according to the world's standards. God wants us to know what is really important, that which is in keeping with his plan and his power.

CONCLUSION

It is so easy for us to get caught up in the world's standards and to look for our salvation in the things the world trusts. We are told that education is the answer to our woes. If we can just educate people about the dangers of some behaviors, they will stop doing them. Experience has proven this false. Neither has spending money on problems solved them. God knows how to change lives and to bring salvation. When we begin valuing his lowly things, life will get better now, and there will be hope for the future. Of such is our Messiah, and we honor his humble beginnings this season.

The Court Case of the Ages
Micah 6:1-8

I love a good court case. The popularity of courtroom television shows such as "Perry Mason," "Law and Order," and "The Practice" indicates that I am not alone. There is excitement in the knowledge that someone is right and someone wrong, and clever people are going to sort it out and bring about justice.

Such is the drama set before us in Micah 6. Court opens with the participants in place. God is the plaintiff, Israel the defendant, and the prophet Micah the attorney for the plaintiff. The mountains serve as the witnesses in this universal court. The charge against Israel? Covenant-breaking.

Micah 2 had pronounced charges and sentence against the wicked land barons. In Micah 3, Israel's corrupt leadership had been sentenced. Finally, the plaintiff brings his complaint against the populace in Micah 6.

Proposition: Our only defense before God is faith in him and faithfulness to his covenant.

I. IN THE GRAND SCHEME OF THINGS, ALL THAT MATTERS IS COVENANT LOYALTY.

A. The plaintiff's spokesman has been told to "Stand up, plead your case before the mountains" (6:1). Micah is to plead the case before the mountains whose roots are the enduring foundations of the earth. These are the mountains that existed when the original covenant was made with Abraham. As such, they are witnesses to the covenant.

B. I have looked at the Grand Canyon and thought about it being there when the Law was given to Moses. I have looked at the Flint Hills of Kansas and gone back in my mind's eye to before the time we know the bison roamed those tall grass prairies, wondering how they looked when David was on his throne. I have watched the ocean swells break on the beaches of Maryland and thought of how they have been doing that since before Christ walked the earth. The mountains of Israel and the God who created them were there before Israel, and they are still there today. They witnessed the covenant when it was first made, and they have witnessed every faithful act of keeping that covenant as well as every unfaithful act of breaking it.

C. How important we think our little speck of time is! How we miss the point! Unless the Lord comes, I'll be gone, and the prairie grass will still wave and the swells will still break on the shore, and what will matter is whether or not I've kept my covenant with my Creator.

II. GOD KEEPS HIS COVENANT PROMISES AND WANTS US TO DO THE SAME.

A. The phrase "My people" is used twice (6:3, 5), which is more a gentle plea than a harsh accusation. Two questions in 6:3 indicate not only God's case against the people but also imply Israel has been rationalizing their behavior. "What have I done to you?" implies that Israel distrusted God. The second question, "How have I burdened you?" also implies that Israel had been murmuring (McComiskey, 2:729). In answer to these questions God reminds them of all he had done for them (rescue from Egypt, giving of the Law and priesthood, and all his saving acts over the years).

B. Today we make our own excuses, offer our own rationalizations. "I would love to be in church, but my financial setbacks make it necessary for me to work seven days a week." "How could a loving God let my family member become terminally ill?" We make our excuses for our own willfulness, but God pleads for us to keep the saving covenant we sealed with him when we called Jesus "Lord."

III. ALL THAT GOD REQUIRES IS FAITHFULNESS TO HIM.

A. Finally a wealthy Israelite steps forward to answer the complaint. Instead of repentant remorse, the respondent answers with questions. He seems to say, "Okay, God, what do you want?" The suggested offerings grow in magnitude to the point of human sacrifice, evidence of arrogant sarcasm. It is an insult to God's gracious protection of his people through the years.

B. Micah's response is an exercise in studied control. He rebukes the respondent with calm truth that carries the weight of centuries of truth and reveals Israel and her spokesman for the callous, blind souls they are. (Read 6:8.) True faith in God and true faithfulness to God will be shown in what "is good," in the integrity of behavior in a just, gentle, and humble walk with God each day. No acts of worship will be beneficial in the absence of this.

CONCLUSION

Hear, you Christians, arise and plead your case before the timeless hills that were here when the covenant promise of salvation in Jesus was made. What has God done that you should take his new covenant so lightly? You respond, "What do you want, God? I'm a church member! I tithe and teach a Sunday school class for you. Do you want my blood too?" "No," he answers, "I want your life to show the highest integrity, evidence of your new life in Christ. I want your demeanor to be gentle. I want you to be humble, ready to obey me without saying you have a better idea."

When God's Patience Runs Out

Jonah and Nahum

"Nineveh has more than a hundred and twenty thousand people who cannot tell their right hand from their left. . . . Should I not be concerned about that great city?" (Jonah 4:11).

"You [Nineveh] will have no descendants to bear your name. I will destroy the carved images and cast idols that are in the temple of your gods. I will prepare your grave, for you are vile" (Nahum 1:14).

These dramatically different statements were made by the same God about the same city, though about a century and a half apart. What happened to make such a difference in the way God spoke of Nineveh? On the one hand, God was explaining to Jonah his reason for caring enough about Nineveh to seek her repentance. One hundred and fifty years later, however, God declared through the prophet Nahum their absolute and permanent condemnation. What had happened? Who had changed, God or Nineveh?

Proposition: God is patient with all people, but his patience has its limits.

I. GOD'S PATIENCE EXTENDS TO ALL CREATION, INCLUDING UNBELIEVING PEOPLE.

A. Nineveh was not merely a nice place that happened not to believe in the true God. According to Jonah 1:2, Nineveh was a great city whose "wickedness has come up before me."

B. Jonah was angry with God. When Nineveh repented in response to his preaching, rather than being elated at his success, he was angry because he knew the patience of God in giving nations time to turn from their sin (4:1, 2).

C. Indeed, throughout the history of Israel, God had been very patient, not only with his people, but also with other nations. He even used other nations to discipline his people. So God noticed the wickedness of Nineveh, cared about that great city, and went to great pains to send his prophet to her.

II. GOD'S PATIENCE LASTS A LONG TIME, BUT IT WILL NOT LAST FOREVER.

A. One hundred and fifty years after Jonah's successful preaching and Nineveh's genuine repentance, Nineveh had forgotten her experience of God's patience. Several generations had lived and died since then. It has been about a century and a half since the Civil War in the United States. How many changes have taken place since then? How much have we forgotten? A nation will change greatly in that period of time.

B. Nahum 1:3 notes, "The Lord is slow to anger and great in power; the Lord will not leave the guilty unpunished." The fact that God is patient does not mean that he will forget or ignore the wickedness of those who turn away from him or turn against him.

C. We human beings are forgetful. We tend to think that God is. We think God's apparent inactivity against us indicates unlimited patience. We have plenty of time to repent. Some day, when we are not so busy or when the pressures aren't so great, we will get around to being righteous. Perhaps if God blessed us a little more we would turn to him sooner. This is dangerous thinking.

III. ONCE GOD'S PATIENCE IS EXHAUSTED, THERE IS NO TURNING BACK.

A. Once his patience is exhausted, we read, "The Lord is a jealous and avenging God; the Lord takes vengeance and is filled with wrath" (Nahum 1:2). (Read Nahum 1 for more statements about the absolute power of a sovereign God.)

B. Once God's patience has ended, the full range of his power will be brought to bear on the offending parties until nothing is left. God promises complete destruction of a country that becomes so wicked as to cause his patience to cease. When God takes action against a nation, there is nothing it can do to stop it (Nahum 1:12, 13).

C. Nahum 3 details the fall of Nineveh. There was no turning back, and there was no help. Unlike the time when God sent Jonah and invited repentance, this time there was no opportunity to repent. It was not an option. There is a point of no return, and Nineveh had crossed it. Her insensitivity to the plight of people under her oppression had gained for her an awful consequence. She ceased to exist.

CONCLUSION

We have seen nations come and go, but since there have been no prophets to interpret these events as God's intervention, we have not related their fall to God's hand. Indeed, it is difficult to know when God's hand is in such events, when it is final, and when it is a temporary setback. I do know there is a spirit abroad in our land that believes, if there is a God, he has endless patience and we may do as we please. He will always give us second and third chances. The experience of Nineveh would not bear that out. God is loving and kind and will give us opportunities to repent. However, those opportunities are not endless. There is a point of no return.

The Divine Warrior

Nahum 1:2-8

It is not easy to get excited about the book of Nahum. At first it seems to be just a prophecy of the vengeance of God against Assyria. It seems to present a picture of a hateful, vindictive God bent on destroying a nation he had formerly forgiven after the preaching of Jonah.

But such a view of Nahum is inaccurate. As McComiskey writes, "The key to the problem is in the opening hymn (1:2-8), which presents the Divine Warrior whose appearance causes the cosmos to quake" (2:776). Nahum seems to look at both sides of Paul's "If God is for us, who can be against us?" (Romans 8:31). The other side of that coin, unspoken by Paul but implied by Nahum, is, "If God is against you, who can stand for you?"

The Israelites experienced both sides of the work of this Divine Warrior. They underwent his discipline and enjoyed his protection. All the forces of Egypt could not prevail against a crew of runaway slaves and their God. Whether it be that or a shepherd boy with a sling or a band of priests blowing trumpets, when the Divine Warrior stands, everyone else bows.

We can also cite times when the Divine Warrior raised troops from unlikely places to discipline his own people. Nowhere is it more graphic than when God told Habakkuk of his intent to bring the Babylonians against Judah. Even then, complete control was in God's hand, so the Babylonian captivity lasted seventy years, as long as he said it would last. And the Divine Warrior always preserved a remnant of the faithful.

**Proposition: God is still the Divine Warrior,
punishing and protecting as he chooses.**

I. GOD INTERVENES IN HUMAN HISTORY AS A PUNISHING WARRIOR.

A. The historical facet of this intriguing concept teaches us something about the nature of God, his immanence and transcendence. Habakkuk is not alone as he complains, "How long, O Lord, must I call for help, but you do not listen? Or cry out to you 'Violence!' but you do not save?" (Habakkuk 1:2). Many are the people who want God to intervene in history on their timetable when he has a timetable of his own.

B. The specifics of the issue in Nahum's day are carried out on the Assyrian city of Nineveh. They have abused God's people as long as he will allow. It will end, for God says it will end. Nahum 2:13 states, "'I am against you,' declares the Lord Almighty, 'I will burn up your chariots in smoke, and the sword will devour your young lions. I will leave you no prey on the earth. The voices of your messengers will no longer be heard.'"

C. His judgment is absolute, complete, and permanent. There is no negotiating, no repenting, no turning back. Assyria has abused God's people as long as he will permit. He has not been unaware or uncaring. Judgment will come soon because God says so.

II. GOD INTERVENES IN INDIVIDUALS' LIVES AS A SPIRITUAL WARRIOR.

A. The Divine Warrior's activity takes a different shape in the New Testament, but it is no less sure, no less sovereign. This is recognized by Peter (Acts 10:36) when he alludes to Nahum 1:15, "Look, there on the mountains, the feet of one who brings good news, who proclaims peace!" The weapons of warfare are different, spiritual rather than military, but they are no less effective. The work looks different because the battle is in a different arena, yet the results are just as sure as when the warriors marched against Nineveh.

B. John the Baptist exhibits the expectations of the people for a warrior Messiah when he speaks of the winnowing fork in his hand. When John questions Jesus from his prison cell, he receives an answer that indicates the change of arena. The battle formerly fought from backs of horses and behind shields is now to be engaged in the spiritual realm and the realm of human hearts and minds as the poor have the gospel preached to them.

C. Every time you turn on your television, read a newspaper, or attend a movie, you are opening your mind to influences from this world. We cannot escape those influences. This is why we all need the Divine Warrior who cannot be defeated, who has already won the battle, to be the one who is our champion.

CONCLUSION

Too often today we attempt to fight God's battles for him using the world's tools. Israel and Judah tried to protect themselves by making alliances with other nations instead of concentrating on being righteous and letting God save them. Today we try to make our nation righteous by lobbying for just laws or bringing political pressure to bear on our opponents.

In the final analysis, all of this will be of no avail. Our efforts should focus on the use of spiritual tools to change the hearts of people while God, the invincible Divine Warrior, sees to the rise and fall of nations and the salvation of his people.

Living by Faith in Hard Times

Habakkuk

World Vision and other care-giving organizations frequently put on television programs showing conditions in other parts of the world. News items frequently feature starving children in the third world countries or crying women in war-torn cities.

I have a hard time watching because they disturb my status quo. They make me uncomfortable because I am not doing anything about it. And they make me angry with people who cause such suffering because of their selfishness or ignorance.

My discomfort is not eased when I look at the home scene. In every city of major proportions, innocent people are being killed by wicked people. Furthermore, rather than encouraging spiritual renewal, which could improve much of this situation, our government makes it harder and harder for the church. To make matters worse, the church sits passively by like a sleeping giant drugged by the numbing fruits of her own self-satisfaction.

My prayer life has changed as I've lost confidence in the church to heal herself or the nation to let the church heal her, so I find myself praying more and more, "God, please do something, anything, in our age to correct these inequities." This is where Habakkuk was in his day. He was thinking about giving up his faith. He was, at the very least, questioning its power to change his nation or world, so he engaged God in argument about it. In his conversation with God, Habakkuk learned to hold on to his faith. He learned there is reason to hope. His striking conversation with God reveals the tremendous benefits of keeping our faith in God, even in difficult times.

**Proposition: When values in our world are up for grabs,
it is worth putting your faith in God.**

I. KEEPING YOUR FAITH IS THE ONLY WAY TO ACHIEVE RIGHTEOUSNESS.

A. Habakkuk 2:4 is the focal point of the book. It sets up the contrast that is played out through the entire book: the contrast between righteous people and evil people.

B. Habakkuk was operating on a common belief—that righteousness is measured by deeds. Note especially Habakkuk's complaint about God's people and their great sinfulness (1:2-4) and his veiled accusation against God: "Why are you silent while the wicked swallow up those more righteous than themselves?" (1:13). Habakkuk was so sure of his position on righteousness that he pressed his complaint by putting himself on a tower to see how God would respond. It is as though Habakkuk wanted to define how we achieve righteousness (2:1).

C. However, no matter what is going on in the world, it isn't what I think about righteousness that counts but what God calls it, and 2:4 states that he will call those who have faith righteous. This is not to be decided by debate. If God is God, he will decide who is righteous and what constitutes righteousness. So, the first benefit of keeping your faith is that God will consider you righteous.

II. KEEPING YOUR FAITH WILL DELIVER YOU FROM THE WOES COMING ON THE UNRIGHTEOUS.

A. God lists five inescapable "woes" to come on the unrighteous, specifically on the one "who piles up stolen goods" (2:6), "who builds his realm by unjust gain" (2:9), "who builds a city with bloodshed" (2:12), "who gives drink to his neighbors . . . till they are drunk" (2:15), "who says to wood, 'Come to life!' Or to lifeless stone, 'Wake up!'" (2:19).

B. God tells Habakkuk that there is no hope for those who seem to have unfair advantages now. Today's "beautiful people" as well as dictators, the wealthy, and oppressors come and go, but God's Word and God's will remain (2:19, 20). So the second benefit of keeping your faith is that it will enable you to escape the inevitable consequences of sin.

III. KEEPING YOUR FAITH WILL GIVE YOU THE ASSURANCE OF SALVATION.

A. Note Habakkuk's journey from doubt to faith. Habakkuk's complaint began, "How long, O Lord, must I call for help, but you do not listen? Or cry out to you, 'Violence!' but you do not save?" (1:2). But this complaint did not lead Habakkuk to give up hope. In 2:1 he states, "I will . . . stand at my watch . . . to see what he will say to me, and what answer I am to give to this complaint."

B. Eventually Habakkuk's faith led him to utter a prayer of confidence to God: "You came out to deliver your people, to save your anointed one" (3:13). One must not miss Habakkuk's movement from hostility to serenity: "I will wait patiently" (3:16).

CONCLUSION

Like Habakkuk, we need to learn to nurture our faith during these hostile times when we are told we are foolish to have faith or when it seems that the rewards for faith are diminishing. We need to learn to say with Habakkuk, "Though the fig tree does not bud and there are no grapes on the vines, though the olive crop fails and the fields produce no food, though there are no sheep in the pen and no cattle in the stalls, yet I will rejoice in the Lord, I will be joyful in God my Savior" (3:17, 18).

Waiting on God

Habakkuk

I can't understand why some things happen as they do. It seems that people with the finances to hire the most famous attorneys are much more likely to go free than those who must be represented by assigned public defenders. I become cynical about justice because neither guilt nor innocence seems to be a factor in the outcome.

In matters of health, it seems that there is no rhyme or reason as to who gets sick and who stays healthy. I know that, statistically, people who practice their Christian faith live longer than those who don't, but this doesn't help much when every day I see devout Christians suffering inexplicable misery.

Tevye, the central character in *Fiddler on the Roof*, struggled to understand these things as well. He complained that he had only daughters and no sons, that he was poor, and that his horse was lame. He couldn't understand why. The story ends with Tevye still not understanding why God let life be so hard.

The prophet Habakkuk was somewhat like Tevye and us in this regard. He began his prophecy by questioning God about why things were as they were. But Habakkuk was different too. By the end of the prophecy Habakkuk had learned to wait on God and, in so doing, had found peace for his soul while the world raged around him.

> **Proposition: We can learn to wait on God by honestly talking to him, then obediently listening to him.**

I. WE NEED TO HONESTLY EXPRESS OUR IMPATIENCE TO GOD.

A. Habakkuk begins his discourse by expressing displeasure with the way God's people are behaving and with the fact that God is not doing anything about it (1:2). He is adamant about God giving a satisfactory answer, so he challenges God to respond: "I will stand at my watch and station myself on the ramparts . . . to see what he will say to me" (2:1).

B. Don't pretend that everything is okay when you seethe inside. That works no better with God than it works with human beings. Pretending everything is good does not make it good.

C. On a number of occasions I have seen Christian people grieving the loss of a child or facing another kind of grave tragedy. It is not uncommon for them to keep silent rather than express their true feelings to God. Until they can come to honest expression to God of their feelings, they do not get rid of the anger. I tell them that even anger expressed honestly to God is an indication of faith. It means that God is so real to them that they can feel and express a full range of emotions in their relationship with him.

II. WE MUST STOP TALKING AND LISTEN TO GOD'S RESPONSE.

A. Throughout Habakkuk 1 God and the prophet conduct a dialogue. Habakkuk complains, God replies, explaining his plans to punish his people through the Babylonian invasion, and Habakkuk counters, expressing his dissatisfaction with God's plans. Finally, in 2:2, Habakkuk says, "Then the Lord replied."

B. God takes charge, and the rest of chapter 2 records God's explanation of how things are. God states his main idea in 2:4—"the righteous will live by his faith"—then follows with a series of woes that are the ultimate end for the wicked. At the end of the day, God's principles will stand!

C. Sometimes we cannot listen to God's Word because we are too busy trying to make it fit our situation rather than altering our situation to fit God's Word. Habakkuk was a careful listener, so he heard that God is the only one of the "gods" who will speak to us: "Woe to him who says to wood, 'Come to life!' Or to lifeless stone, 'Wake up!' Can it give guidance?" (2:19). God has spoken. Don't rationalize his Word but listen to it, for "the Lord is in his holy temple; let all the earth be silent before him" (2:20).

III. WE SHOULD ADJUST OUR EXPECTATIONS AS NEEDED.

A. Chapter 3 records Habakkuk's prayer. It is one of the most beautiful statements of faith, humility, and trust to be found anywhere. Habakkuk has progressed from brusque inquisitor to compliant servant by remembering what God has done, both for him and for his nation.

B. It is a human tendency to see only the immediate situation. God is concerned with much more than our little speck of time and space. When we begin to see the big picture of God's dealing with humanity throughout history, we get a better perspective on his actions and begin to see his justice.

C. Finally, from the one who had accused God of not acting properly, come the faith-filled declarations of 3:13 and 18, "You came out to deliver your people, to save your anointed one. . . . I will be joyful in God my Savior."

CONCLUSION

Engage God in honest conversation through his Word. Listen honestly. Humbly surrender your will to his. Then you, like Habakkuk, will discover peace even in the most difficult of situations.

The Day of the Lord

Zephaniah 1:1-18

Sometimes it is hard to know what to think about Judgment Day. There are days when I think it would be a pretty good idea for it to come NOW! But more often life is good enough that I don't want the day of the Lord to come for a long time.

The Minor Prophets contain many references to the day of the Lord. Amos, for example, said, "Woe to you who long for the day of the Lord! Why do you long for the day of the Lord? That day will be darkness, not light" (5:18). Or, "prepare to meet your God, O Israel!" (4:12). In Obadiah 4, God says to Edom, "Though you soar like the eagle and make your nest among the stars, from there I will bring you down."

Edom, Israel, Judah, and other nations of that day appeared to believe they could make their own way in the world. They sought to assure success through alliances with other nations, successful harvests, or by military might. As long as they were successful, they thought, the day of the Lord would be good to them. Zephaniah indicates that this is not necessarily the case.

**Proposition: Even though we may not expect it,
our ever-watchful God will judge all people, including his own.**

I. GOD WILL JUDGE ALL PEOPLE, INCLUDING THOSE WHO CLAIM TO BE HIS.

A. Zephaniah begins by announcing God's judgment on the whole earth because of the unfaithfulness of Judah, especially her priests (1:2-6). Then, in 1:7-14a, he pronounces judgment on Judah before returning to declare judgment on the rest of humanity in 1:14b-18. What would cause God to bring judgment?

People devoted themselves to false gods (1:5). Officials devoted themselves to the acquisition of material possessions, especially foreign (i.e., imported and expensive) clothes (1:8). Merchants devoted their lives to trading and bartering (1:11), while the rich gave themselves to acquiring real estate (1:13).

B. God's judgment will interrupt the human pursuit of material possessions, the pursuits that give them confidence in their future and ease from worry about their old age. God says they will neither inhabit the houses they build nor drink the wine from their vineyards.

C. Is that it? Is it just the pursuit of material things that has God so disturbed that he is going to end it all, both for those who claim to serve him and those who don't? Surely there is more to it than that. Zephaniah 1:17 is quite graphic as people walk like the blind and have their blood "poured out like dust and their entrails like filth." That is a fairly horrible description of what will happen.

II. GOD WILL JUDGE THE WORLD EVEN THOUGH PEOPLE DON'T EXPECT IT.

A. It is, of course, sin that leads God to bring judgment, but what might I be doing to hasten the day? According to Zephaniah 1:5, God's people raise his fury as much as the officials and princes in 1:8.

B. We don't expect God to do anything! It is people who have professed faith in God and who are carrying out some form of worship who "neither seek the Lord nor inquire of him" (1:6; see also 1:12). It is people who do not see God involved in their lives, who do not see him immanent in this world who bring on his wrath. Perhaps it is better to see God acting and argue against it than not to see him present at all.

III. KNOWING THAT GOD IS WATCHING SHOULD AFFECT OUR BEHAVIOR.

A. The Israelites at Mount Sinai waiting for Moses to return with God's law built the golden calf for various reasons, among which was the belief that God was not going to do a thing.

B. Today we find within Christianity many who seem to think that God is totally transcendent, inactive in human affairs. It is very dangerous to believe, think, or act as if we are alone here. It is not just the question of whether God will be immanent to meet my needs. It is more a matter of understanding that God is watching my behavior, the genuineness of my worship, and the things that I pursue to give me confidence for life. Do I behave as if I believe he acts in this world? Do I make decisions according to God's Word and will or according to what will give me "happiness" or meet my "needs"?

C. Every time God's people began living as though, "The Lord will do nothing, either good or bad" (1:12), God sent his prophets to warn them that he would not have it. Whether it is Habakkuk wondering aloud how God could use the Babylonians to punish Judah or Amos warning Israel that God would use the Assyrians to punish them or Zephaniah stating the general principle that God watches and intervenes in human history, the message is consistent.

CONCLUSION

The world at large, and even some Christians, shows little sign of expecting God to do anything significant, for good or ill, in our day. That is dangerous! Let us heed the message and warning of Zephaniah.

Readiness

Zephaniah 2:1-4

Cramming for exams, last-minute Christmas shopping, preparing income taxes just before they are due—all these events speak of the prevalent human tendency to procrastinate. Jesus addressed it in the parable of the maidens awaiting the marriage feast, and the prophets addressed it as well.

But when Jesus and the prophets addressed the problem, it did not concern an approaching exam, holiday, or tax deadline but the day of reckoning. In some cases this "day of the Lord" refers to God's final judgment, while in others it relates to a temporal judgment, such as the fall of nations or the experience of some calamity. In either case, however, the need for readiness remains the same.

Zephaniah speaks on the subject of readiness for God's judgment in 2:1-4. The idea of being ready for any judgment or evaluation is not a new idea, but Zephaniah presents it in such interesting imagery that it bears close examination.

For some, the direct approach of Amos, who simply said, "Prepare to meet your God, O Israel!" (4:12b), may be most effective. For others, Zephaniah's picturesque call to prepare may be what causes change. Whatever works for you, you will be wise to hear the messages of Jesus and the prophets and procrastinate no more.

Proposition: We should prepare ourselves now for the coming day of the Lord.

I. PREPARING FOR THE DAY OF THE LORD BEGINS WITH REPENTANCE.

A. Zephaniah 1:18 and 2:2, 3 make it clear that the prophet is speaking of the judgment of God on a sinful world. We could spend hours identifying the similarities between the sinfulness of that day and the sinfulness of ours, then predict that the judgment of God will come soon. But since we cannot accurately predict time, it is more important to do something to assure our readiness for it whenever it might come.

B. Zephaniah calls the people of God to come together for repentance and then repeats the word "before" three times: "before the appointed time arrives," "before the fierce anger of the Lord comes upon you," and "before the day of the Lord's wrath comes upon you" (2:2). The message is, "Repent before the storm of God's wrath comes upon you." The picture is that of people waiting during the eerie silence before a storm, ignoring the fact that they may soon be driven like chaff in a hurricane-force wind.

When the National Hurricane Center issues a warning for a certain area, the weather at the time is often calm. It is hard to believe that devastation is on the way. Inevitably, some people steadfastly and stubbornly refuse to evacuate the area. They are warned that once the storm hits there will be no rescue, for even rescue workers won't venture out. The storm of God's wrath against sin isn't something that may come someday. Like an asteroid in a disaster movie, it is hurtling toward us, and the fact that we do not know its exact course does not diminish its certainty.

II. PREPARING FOR THE DAY OF THE LORD CONTINUES WITH SEEKING GOD.

A. While the word "before" echoed through 2:2, the cry to "seek" reverberates in 2:3: "Seek the Lord. . . . Seek righteousness, seek humility." While the former has to do with timing, the latter is a matter of action. Awareness of the need to act should get us moving. Note that this is a cry to God's people. There is need for them, too, to be ready.

B. The repetition of "seeking" does not teach that there are three separate things that must be sought, as though Zephaniah were providing a list of rules or a formula for passing muster on the day of God's wrath. Rather, this is a poetic form for emphasis. We need to be aware not only that we are waiting for the day of the Lord but that action on our part is required as we wait.

C. One way to ready ourselves is to actively pursue God through righteousness and humility. It is admitting that the day of the Lord will require something of me according to the standard of God's righteousness. It takes humility to accept this. While much of our society today thinks that God will save people based on their own standard of goodness, the humble person accepts that it will be God's standard of righteousness, not our own, by which we will stand or fall on the day of judgment.

CONCLUSION

We were parked along the shoulder of an icy Pennsylvania road one January evening in 1989. We had stopped to help some people whose car had slid into the ditch. Out of nowhere, and with no sound to warn us, we were struck from behind by a car sliding sideways at a high rate of speed. The impact made a loud "bam," and our van was propelled across two lanes of highway to the opposite shoulder, about one hundred yards down the road. For a few minutes, there was an eerie silence. It was as if nothing had happened and we were the only people for miles around. The driver of the car that hit us was dead. Suddenly and silently he faced eternity, with no time to do anything before going. No time to seek any qualities or character traits to take with him. It was done.

Before that day comes for you, seek righteousness and humility that you may be hidden from danger when the day of God's reckoning comes.

Going Forward When Times Are Hard

Haggai

Do you ever feel that the harder you work, the harder things get? Jeremiah refers to the people of God as having dug cisterns that are cracked (2:13). In a similar way, Haggai characterizes the feeling as follows: "You earn wages, only to put them in a purse with holes in it" (1:6).

Such was the situation of the people of Judah in the days of Haggai the prophet. Having returned from Babylonian exile, they had put great effort into rebuilding their homes, but they had not yet rebuilt the temple. Needless to say, God was not pleased with them, so he frustrated all their efforts. Crops were bad, there was not enough rain, and things weren't going well for most of the people. To make matters worse, the harder life got, the harder it was to get enthused about building anything, let alone something unnecessary for day-to-day existence.

Then along came Haggai, a stern taskmaster who gave no quarter. He didn't join them in their self-pity but chided them for their lack of resolve to do God's bidding. He explained that their difficulties were related to their lack of movement toward God's goals, that they desperately needed to build the temple. Haggai identified the obstacles to their progress and then helped them overcome those obstacles.

**Proposition: God's people need to recognize and overcome
all obstacles that keep them from serving God.**

I. MATERIALISM CAN PRESENT AN OBSTACLE TO SPIRITUAL PROGRESS (1:1-6).

A. The people of Judah were held back by materialism. They said they wanted to build the house of God, but it wasn't time yet. They had time to build their paneled houses, but they needed a little more material security before giving what it would cost to build the temple. The temple would have to wait.

B. It is the nature of materialism that there is never enough. Capitalism thrives on this reality. We hope to have jobs with possibility for advancement, buy "starter homes" so we can "move up" later, and trade in perfectly fine older cars for new ones. Capitalism's very existence depends on a growing market and growing productivity, while we all enjoy the fruits of materialism.

C. The pressures of materialism distract us from endeavors that are not material in nature: reading, praying, lounging under a shade tree with a tall lemonade and watching children play. The lure of materialism causes us to say, "Tithing would be a good thing, but I'm so deeply in debt it isn't possible for me now." So we feel guilty or offended when the preacher teaches that we should tithe or give "over and above" gifts for a new building fund. Such were the people of Judah in Haggai's day.

D. But the people listened when Haggai told them that God had been holding back his blessings because of their materialism (1:7-11). They stopped trusting in their own abilities, laid aside materialism, and began building the temple. Materialism is conquered by trusting God—not by finally getting enough.

II. TRADITIONALISM CAN ALSO RETARD THE PROGRESS OF GOD'S PEOPLE (2:1-9).

A. When the people began to work on the temple, some were paralyzed by the realization that the new temple would not be as glorious as the old one that Solomon had built. Rather than seeing the temple as a means to facilitate the worship of God, they saw it as an end in itself. Because of that, they faltered in their task.

B. Have you ever found yourself feeling as they did? "It will never be as good as it was in the good old days, so why try?" We could debate whether the good old days were really that good, but we have all shared those feelings at some time or other.

Why don't we like to learn new songs? They aren't like the good old songs! Why don't we want to relocate the church? It won't stir the same memories in a new location! As Joe Ellis points out in his book, *The Church on Purpose,* traditions are wonderful and helpful for many things, but they are "means" to achieve "ends." When they become ends in themselves, they hold us back from our purpose.

III. LOSS OF HOPE OFFERS A SERIOUS OBSTACLE TO ANY PROGRESS AT ALL (2:20-23).

A. Existentialism states that what exists is all that there is. Existence, not essence, is the driving force. Such a view is the mother of humanism, which trusts only in human ability and ingenuity and ultimately ends up in hopelessness.

B. The people of Judah had lost hope that God would act through them. Haggai needed to remind them they were a part of the onward marching plan of God and that he was waiting to act through a faithful people.

CONCLUSION

There is no lack of great purposes to achieve for God today. Often we hold back because we can't afford it, we can't do it with style, it will take too long, or people are not ready for it. God says to give up these things and just start! See if he won't help us!

God's Important House

Zechariah

Haggai, Malachi, and Zechariah each played a key role in the reconstruction of the temple after the Babylonian exile. Each seemed to have a different role in the prophetic vision that accompanied this project. Haggai prodded and coaxed God's people with the practical aspects of building the temple. He met each objection to convince them that their excuses did not release them from responsibility to obey God in building the temple.

Malachi was the seer who took responsibility to see that they used the temple with integrity. This was not to be a place for empty religious ritual growing out of cold hearts and slipshod religion. The people of Judah were not to despise God in their use of his house.

Zechariah, who had been sent back from captivity after Haggai was already in Jerusalem, came to shed yet a third light on the project as he vigorously urged the people to get on with the temple construction.

Why was the building of the temple so important? We don't want to question the importance of that which God considers important, but it can only deepen our appreciation for the house of God if we understand his reasons. It is from Zechariah that we gain important and useful insights into God's perspective on his house.

**Proposition: A house of worship was necessary
for the proper development of a spiritual religion.**

I. THE BUILDING OF GOD'S HOUSE USHERED IN THE AGE OF A NEW PROMISE (1:18-21).

A. In Zechariah's vision, four craftsmen destroy the four horns representing the nations that had "scattered Judah, Israel and Jerusalem" (1:19). Although one might expect mighty symbols of war for the destruction of nations, there is a new age coming that will not depend on warfare nor be led by judges or kings.

B. God is angry with the nations (1:15), but his main goal is not their destruction but the building up and the prospering of his city, Jerusalem (1:16, 17). God's people will be blessed to rise from the dust of their captivity with the mighty temple of God's presence to convey the promise.

II. THE TEMPLE GIVES A PHYSICAL REPRESENTATION OF GOD'S PRESENCE (2:10).

A. Instead of an army that God empowers, there is now to be a house in which God dwells. This house, the temple, will be the center for spiritual renewal and awakening. Zechariah 2:10 says, "'Shout and be glad, O Daughter of Zion. For I am coming, and I will live among you,' declares the Lord."

Some today look forward to building the temple again on the original site in Jerusalem. They see it as a symbol of the presence of the nation of Israel. But in the day of Zechariah the temple was to be a symbol of the presence of God.

B. Although we do not depend on any object for the presence of God, and while churches throughout the land are not thought of as temples, it is possible that we may have gone too far in the individualization and the privatization of faith in America. Perhaps we would do well to see our houses of worship as more than "campuses," "plants," "units," or "family-life centers." Is it possible they could become representations of God's presence once again?

C. I'm not advocating making idols of church buildings. I've also seen situations in which churches seemed to be in the church-building business. In both cases the buildings become the objects of adoration and pride. God is incidental in such situations. Instead, I am advocating the presence of the church building as a silent but constant visual reminder to a community that the people of God have dedicated this space to him. Therefore, they care for it with loving hands and use it for events that bring honor to his name.

III. THE HOUSE OF GOD REPRESENTS GOD'S POWER TO SAVE PEOPLE (6:9-14).

A. Here Zechariah is told to fashion a crown of gold and silver and place it on the head of Joshua, the high priest. This mingling of the kingly role (crown) with the office of priest is unusual. The fact that this crowned priest represents one named "Branch," who will combine the roles of priest and king, is indicative of its prophetic reference to the Messiah. Even as God's presence is promised immediately in the rebuilt temple, his incarnate presence is foretold in the Branch.

B. There is messianic prediction present in the whole process. God's love for his people creates within him a desire to be present among the faithful, whether in the tabernacle with the Israelites under Moses' leadership, in the temple with the returned exiles, in the Messiah during his presence on earth, or in his future return for the faithful of the present age.

CONCLUSION

God has taken great pains throughout the centuries to assure the faithful of his presence and of his desire to save. Let us conduct our lives in his church in such a way as to show his presence to our world today.

Protection by a Watchful Father

Zechariah 9:1-10

It is always difficult to preach about the triumphal entry. Nevertheless, I've always wanted to break through the clichés to feel some of the excitement of the people who laid the palm branches and coats in the path of the donkey on which Jesus rode.

Zechariah 9:1-10 recounts the history of many of Israel's enemies, a history that culminates in the triumphal entry. Verses 1-7 recite the fall of city-states in an order and a way that closely resembles the march of Alexander the Great through that part of the world in 333 B.C. Verses 6 and 7, for example, promise an end to Philistia, that long-standing thorn in the flesh to God's people. The Philistines had been Israel's nemesis since the times of the Judges. Then we seem to jump to the prophecy of the triumphal entry. What is the prophet doing here? What does this mean?

Proposition: Jesus' triumphal entry culminates centuries of God's promises to his people.

I. GOD FIRST PROMISES TO PUNISH ISRAEL'S ENEMIES (9:1-7).

A. Just as Israel belongs to God, so also do all cities and nations. Therefore, the surrounding powers that had oppressed Israel for so many generations would be dispensed with by God (9:1-6). If, indeed, the order of the fall of these places does coincide with the march of Alexander the Great across Palestine, and his march was a partial fulfillment of this prophecy, it presents a new perspective on Alexander's conquests.

B. Verse 7 is indicative of more than simple military victory. There is the horrid picture of Philistia as an animal with blood on its mouth and the bits of meat from its pagan sacrifices clinging to its teeth. Not only will God take away the pride of Philistia, he will also take away her pagan practices. This is history to us, but it was personal to the people of Israel. They recalled the Philistines and Samson, the Philistines and David, and many other trials brought on them by the Philistines.

C. Archaeology has uncovered little of glory and beauty from Philistia. Military might was their forte, and when that was destroyed, they had little legacy to leave to the world.

II. GOD PROMISES THAT HE WILL ALWAYS GUARD HIS PEOPLE (9:8).

A. God promises in 9:8 that, after destroying the Philistine cities and bringing that nation down to serve Israel, he will guard his people against oppressors. What a promise! God himself will stand guard at the gate of the Israelites. Since Israel's guard was also God over the nations, Israel could rest secure under his protection.

B. As the armies of the conquering forces marched by in their conquest of the neighboring powers, God stood guard over his people to protect them from being banished from the earth. As McComiskey notes, "This section looks far beyond the conquests of Alexander to envision the people of God in all ages. Thus, God protects his people today" (3:1163).

C. While God is aware of the nations that are under his power, he also keeps his eyes on his people. He is constantly aware, at all times, of what is happening with them and will not forget his covenant with them even though they may sometimes forget.

III. GOD'S FINAL PROMISE IS THE VICTORY OF THEIR KING (9:9, 10).

A. Words such as "triumphant," "victorious," and "humble" are very familiar to people who have been to a few Palm Sunday services. And so it should be, for this is the promise of the King who will enter Jerusalem in peace and victory. The New Testament makes it clear that this section of Zechariah is prophetic of the Palm Sunday event.

B. Furthermore, there is the promise in 9:10a of the reuniting of Israel and Judah. Ephraim (Israel) and Jerusalem (Judah) will no longer brandish weapons of war. Instead, this new victorious King will declare "peace to the nations. His rule will extend from sea to sea and from the River to the ends of the earth" (9:10).

C. Here is the picture: The promise of 9:8b that no oppressor shall again overrun them was not fulfilled during the history of Israel and Judah up to the time of Jesus, so the people longed for it to be kept. In Jesus' triumphal entry they saw the keeping of the promise of the centuries. What they did not know was that the promise was also that the kingdom would be in the hearts of people of all nations, not in a territory on the earth and not just among blood descendants of Abraham.

CONCLUSION

No wonder "the stones would cry out" if the people were silent. God's promise was being fulfilled, and realizing this, their excitement could not be contained. Yet the presence of Christ is not about power. It is about the keeping of God's promises.

Ready or Not

Zechariah 9:1-10

I've always been fascinated by the behavior of people in Jerusalem during the last week of Jesus' life on earth. On Palm Sunday they crowded around him shouting, "Hosanna to the Son of David!" (Matthew 21:9) as they put palm branches and coats in his path. Then, just a few days later, the crowds in the same city, perhaps some of the same people, shouted with equal vigor, "Crucify him!" (Matthew 27:22).

Although Matthew explains that the priests and elders persuaded the crowds to ask for Barabbas's release and Jesus' crucifixion, I still can't shake a certain haunting feeling. I think the feeling comes from self-doubt. I wonder what it would have been like to be there. Would I have been in the crowd on Palm Sunday, then later in the crowd crying for his death?

There is help in Zechariah's prophecy for those who agonize over the question. This prophecy was available to the people who made the triumphal entry what it was. But I doubt that they were thinking of it when they waved the palms and set their coats before the King.

Proposition: God will keep his promises, but perhaps not as we hope or expect.

I. THE PEOPLE OF JESUS' DAY EXPECTED GOD TO SEND A WARRIOR KING.

A. If they had thought of the prophecy of Zechariah, it would have been easy to say "amen" to 9:1-7, to what God had promised in the prophecy of the fall of Palestinian cities, especially those of the Philistines. Then they would have been able to study the march of Alexander the Great through Palestine in 333 B.C. and rejoice because God kept his promises.

The pride of the Philistines, those people who were a thorn in the flesh to God's people for centuries, had now been vanquished. The horrors of their military exploits were all they had left for a legacy, for the God of Israel had brought them down.

B. Then the people, if they cared to take a break from waving the palms, could have taken a look at Zechariah 9:8 and reflected on God's watchfulness over them. They could read that he would become the guard of their house and watch with his own eyes. They could marvel at how their nation had been preserved to that very day. There had been oppressors, and even then they were under Roman domination. Nevertheless, the sanctity of their nation had been preserved. God had kept them a nation, had protected their temple, and had continued to be with them through thick and thin.

But even with all this to remember and point to, they did not stay loyal to Jesus. A few days later they were ready to crucify him. What happened?

C. The mystery goes on. If they had stopped to reflect, they could have recalled Zechariah 9:9 and realized that they were doing exactly what the prophecy commanded. They were rejoicing greatly over God's king. It was so exciting and intriguing. He was king, yet he was not coming in military victory but in a humble manner. They could handle that. A humble, benevolent monarch would be good—and they would be done with Rome! God was keeping his promise! It was a day to rejoice.

D. Like them, we rejoice over God's kept promises. Sometimes we even rejoice over vague promises we consider to be kept. We are more inclined to extol God's "blessings" in a general way without recounting them because that is what good Christians do. At the triumphal entry the people had something specific to celebrate. God was fulfilling a promise made over five hundred years earlier.

II. THE PEOPLE OF JESUS' DAY DID NOT EXPECT A SPIRITUAL KINGDOM.

A. The day passed, the night came; then the dawn and another day and another. This Jesus didn't act like their humble king, overturning tables in the temple, giving conciliatory statements about Roman taxes but scathing verbal attacks on their leaders! No one expected this kind of behavior. He was just going to stir things up and prompt Rome to come down on them and take away what little freedom they had left. No! He had to be stopped, and they had to go into damage control.

B. But how is all this going to help me be sure I wouldn't have been a turncoat, or more importantly that I won't be one in the future? The key is Zechariah 9:10. Jesus' kingdom is to be a dominion of peace, a reign for all nations, a spiritual kingdom. It will no longer be about war and might and weapons. It will be about grace and forgiveness and being born again into his nature.

CONCLUSION

The people of Jesus' day turned on him because they were ready for God to keep his promises, but they weren't prepared to accept what that meant. If God is really my God, and if I am really the kind of believer who won't turn, I need to be sure that my faith is of the kind that will accept not only the keeping of the promises but also what the keeping of those promises means. If I have to change, so be it. Then, and only then, can I have confidence that I will not turn as did the crowds after Palm Sunday.

Qualities of
Faithfulness
Malachi

There is a tendency today to compartmentalize life, to say that one's performance in one area of life has nothing to do with one's performance in another area of life. Some say the fact that a man is gay should have nothing to do with his opportunity to teach young children. Sexual orientation and occupation are distinct and separate compartments that have no bearing on one another.

Most conservatives of Judeo-Christian background are uncomfortable with such compartmentalization. However, in some other circumstances, perhaps we are just as prone to compartmentalize. Does a pastor have to be perfect? Obviously not. But how much sin can we tolerate before a pastor should be disqualified from spiritual leadership? The answer to that question varies widely among Christians, and the variance is due, to some extent, to the amount of compartmentalization we allow.

The prophet Malachi comes to the people of Judah after the Babylonian captivity and the rebuilding of the temple. Haggai had successfully prodded the people into completing the temple. Now Malachi attempts to sting the conscience of Judah's priesthood and people about the quality of their worship. Haggai dealt with trusting God for the resources to build his house. Malachi deals with honoring God in using his house.

How does this relate to compartmentalization? The people and priests wanted to receive the benefits of faith in God without reciprocal behavior. For instance, being a priest was one compartment. Marriage was another, and teaching was another. They wanted a priesthood whether or not the priests were faithful husbands and teachers.

Malachi addressed this tendency to put faith in God and faithfulness to God into two different compartments, which is apropos for today. Many claim they are "saved by faith" while they continue to lead their lives as they please. Malachi's prophecy reveals insights into the impossibility of valid faith without faithfulness.

Proposition: We cannot have a valid faith without being faithful.

I. WE CANNOT HAVE FAITH IN ANOTHER UNLESS WE OURSELVES ARE FAITHFUL.

   A. To have faith in someone else is to have confidence in that person's abilities, character, integrity, and the like. We believe we can trust that person's word or performance. Faithfulness, on the other hand, is a quality of one's character that causes one to be trustworthy. Faithfulness is the quality that causes others to have faith in the one who is faithful.

B. The people of Malachi's day, especially priests, wanted to practice faith without faithfulness. They went through the motions and wanted the benefits of faith in God, but they offered improper sacrifices, promoted incorrect teaching, and were unfaithful in their marriage covenants (2:8-12). They complained when they received no benefit from their religious practices. God said it was because they were not faithful people.

II. GOD IS FAITHFUL TO US, SO WE WHO HAVE FAITH MUST BE FAITHFUL TO HIM.

A. We have already established that faithfulness is the characteristic that causes others to have faith in one. God reminds the people that he made a covenant with Levi, which they both kept (2:4-7). God was true to his word in promises to punish as well to bless (as with his dealings with Esau, 1:2-5).

B. But God was upset with Judah. He had kept his covenants with them, yet they had not kept their part of the covenant. They wanted benefits as a return for practicing what they perceived as "the faith" even when they were unfaithful.

C. Often we preach sermons on small bits of the message of Malachi: "God hates divorce" or "Will a man rob God?" Yet these were only symptoms of Judah's breakdown in faithfulness. Words such as "love" and "honor" stand in stark contrast to "despise," "pollute," "profane," and "hate." For example, God asks, "If I am a father, where is the honor due me? If I am a master, where is the respect due me?" (1:6). The Lord questions the "faith" of a people who claim to have faith in him but who do not show faithfulness to him (2:10-12).

D. The people felt that God's demands were a "burden" (1:13) and flooded "the Lord's altar with tears" because God no longer accepted their offerings (2:13). But the problem was not with God. God had been faithful to them. They, on the other hand, would not experience God's approval and acceptance until they proved the authenticity of their faith by living faithfully before him.

CONCLUSION

The people of Judah wanted to compartmentalize faith and faithfulness. They wanted the benefits of faith while they offered their sacrifices, gave their offerings, made their covenants, and obeyed their religious teaching in the easiest way. God cannot see the "faith" of a people who are not faithful by nature and practice. God must be able to count on us as we count on him. Otherwise we profane our worship and despise the house of our God. We are faithless to our commitments to marriage and to teaching our children. We cannot compartmentalize faith and faithfulness!

Looking for the Sunrise

Malachi 3:16–4:6

Solomon concluded Ecclesiastes by saying, "Now all has been heard; here is the conclusion of the matter: Fear God and keep his commandments, for this is the whole duty of man. For God will bring every deed into judgment, including every hidden thing, whether it is good or evil" (Ecclesiastes 12:13, 14).

Now as the sun sets on the Old Testament revelation and the last prophet pens his last words, one thousand years of recording God's words comes to a close. Malachi probably was not aware that the penning of his last words would close the door for over four hundred years of silence. Still, his last words bear tremendous insight and prepare people in all ages to wait for the sun to rise on the next "day of the Lord."

The day of the Lord is an important concept throughout the prophets. Amos warned Israel not to look forward to the day of the Lord: "Woe to you who long for the day of the Lord! . . . That day will be darkness, not light" (Amos 5:18).

In Malachi's day, great numbers of God's people had stopped fearing him. They thought that God would not act either to bless or to curse, so they went their own ways. They did this because they wanted to see God do something to compel their belief in him. As always, however, there was a faithful remnant who revered the Lord. To these two groups of people, God, through Malachi, spoke the last words before the long silence, words of despair and hope, judgment and blessing, scorching fire and beautiful sunrise. The difference was not in what God did but in what his people did. Malachi's last words give us the keys to approaching the day of the Lord with joyous anticipation.

> **Proposition: The day of the Lord will be a great sunrise**
> **for those who fear, serve, and trust in the Lord.**

I. WE SHOULD REVERE THE LORD AND HONOR HIS NAME (3:16, 17; 4:2).

A. The first key to making the day of the Lord a great sunrise is to revere the Lord and honor his name. Many in Judah were scorning God for not taking better care of them, but there was a remnant who held God in high honor and did not need him to do things on command in order for them to believe in him. The first were like those today who say, "If there is a God, why does he let people starve?" Behind this seemingly honest question is a spirit that does not fear God, trust his judgment, or honor his name. This spirit feels ready to call God to account any time for any reason. But those who fear God trust him even when they cannot understand his actions.

B. The faithful of Malachi's day wrote their names in a book as a record that they trusted and feared God. It was a public statement of their faith in God and their willingness to trust him at all times. These are the ones, God says, for whom the rising sun after the silence of night will be a blessed event bringing healing to his people.

II. WE SHOULD SERVE THE LORD FAITHFULLY (3:18).

A. The second key to making the day of the Lord a great sunrise is to serve the Lord. The righteous are those who fear and serve God. The wicked are those who do not fear and serve God but who stand in judgment of his actions. People need not have done horrible acts to be counted among the wicked. On the other hand, people need not have done heroic acts to be counted among the righteous.

B. The way we will be able to see the difference between the righteous and the wicked will be by watching what happens when the day of the Lord comes. The rising sun of that day will be a scorching heat that consumes the wicked and turns them to ashes. However, it will be a "sun of righteousness . . . with healing in its wings" (4:2) for those who fear and serve God. The imagery continues in 4:3 as the righteous cavort like calves released into the barnyard, their feet grinding the ashes of the wicked who have been charred by the sun.

III. WE SHOULD REMEMBER GOD'S PROMISES (4:4-6).

A. The third key to making the day of the Lord a great sunrise is to remember the covenant with Moses at Sinai. The wicked have forgotten what God has done and over how many years he did it. They want him to act now, in their time, to do their bidding. They forget that he has acted again and again.

B. The promise of the return of Elijah follows. The key to having confidence in new promises is by remembering old promises kept. Moses and Elijah come together (as they will again at the transfiguration) to remind the people of God's faithfulness through the Law and the Prophets. We now know the promise of Elijah's return to be the prophecy of John the Baptist, and Christ's advent was "that great and dreadful day" (4:5). It was great and dreadful in its power, a blessing to those who believe, a stumbling block to unbelievers.

CONCLUSION

When the sun rose in Christ on the day of the Lord, God spoke for another fifty years. Now, the sun has set on his revelation for nearly two thousand years. Some are skeptical about another "day of the Lord" that is promised in a second coming. Believe it will come, as a scorching fire to the wicked and as a great sunrise to those who fear his name. Serve him, and remember what he has done.